The Quilting Experience

A Celebration of Community and Patchwork Patterns

Victoria Findlay Wolfe
Foreword by Meg Cox

Copyright © 2024 by Victoria Findlay Wolfe

Library of Congress Control Number: 2024931501

All rights reserved. No part of this work may be reproduced or used in any form or by any means—graphic, electronic, or mechanical, including photocopying or information storage and retrieval systems—without written permission from the publisher.

The scanning, uploading, and distribution of this book or any part thereof via the Internet or any other means without the permission of the publisher is illegal and punishable by law. Please purchase only authorized editions and do not participate in or encourage the electronic piracy of copyrighted materials.

The patterns and designs in this book may be used to make items for personal use only. They may not be used for personal profit nor public display without written permission from the publisher.

"Schiffer Craft" and the crane logo are registered trademarks of Schiffer Publishing, Ltd.

Designed by Ashley Millhouse & Danielle D. Farmer
Cover design by Danielle D. Farmer

Photographs by Jason Langheine, with the below exceptions:
Contributors' snapshots in "Threads" stories.
Photographs by Alan Radom: Front cover top & bottom; pages 4, 11, 22, 25, 26, 190, 198, 201, 203, 205, 208, 210, 218, 222, 224.

Type set in Arima Madurai / Expressway / Playfair Display

ISBN: 978-0-7643-6807-3
Printed in China

Published by Schiffer Craft
An imprint of Schiffer Publishing, Ltd.
4880 Lower Valley Road
Atglen, PA 19310
Phone: (610) 593-1777; Fax: (610) 593-2002
Email: Info@schifferbooks.com
Web: www.schifferbooks.com

For our complete selection of fine books on this and related subjects, please visit our website at www.schifferbooks.com. You may also write for a free catalog.

Schiffer Publishing's titles are available at special discounts for bulk purchases for sales promotions or premiums. Special editions, including personalized covers, corporate imprints, and excerpts, can be created in large quantities for special needs. For more information, contact the publisher.

We are always looking for people to write books on new and related subjects. If you have an idea for a book, please contact us at proposals@schifferbooks.com.

Other Schiffer Craft Books on Related Subjects:

HERstory Quilts: A Celebration of Strong Women, Susanne Miller Jones, ISBN 978-0-7643-5460-1

Portable Patchwork: The Women Pioneers of the Original Quick & Easy Quilting Method, with Projects for Today, Pamela Weeks, ISBN 978-0-7643-6202-6

The Quilting Power Grid: A Design Skillbook for Beginning Modern Quilters, with 50 Example Projects, Sandra Sider, ISBN 978-0-7643-6550-8

Contents

Acknowledgments	5
Foreword by Meg Cox	6
Introduction	9
Planning	18

CHAPTER 1: Identity	31
CHAPTER 2: Traditions	43
CHAPTER 3: Comfort and Healing	57
CHAPTER 4: Connection	71
CHAPTER 5: Aging	85
CHAPTER 6: Teaching and Lessons Learned	97
CHAPTER 7: Friendship	111
CHAPTER 8: Travel	125
CHAPTER 9: Remembering and Grief	139
CHAPTER 10: Food	155
CHAPTER 11: Celebration	165
CHAPTER 12: New Adventures	179

The Experience Quilt Construction	190
Additional Projects	
Spirited Star Quilt	198
Loops, Lines, & Dimensions Quilt	201
Loops & Lines Quilt	203
Floris Ombre Quilt	205
Floris Lattice Quilt	208
Traveling Hearts Quilt	210
Facets Block Pillow	215
Bestie Block Pillow	217
Jubilate Quilt	218
Constant Classic Quilt	222
Facets Quilt	224

Saving Our Stories:	
The Work of the Quilt Alliance	227
Resources	230
Templates	231

Acknowledgments

This book is for my dear friends who are always up for sharing stories and laughing with me: Kim Hryniewicz, Helen Beall, Earamichia Brown, Deb Hunter, Maureen Clark, and Shelly Pagliai. These friendships mean the world to me.

Shouting out heaps of gratitude to Kim Hryniewicz, Tony Jacbobson, Shelly Pagliai, Carol Wesolik, Edie McGinnis, Meg Cox, Amy Milne, Frances O'Roark Dowell, Emma Parker, Julie Hirt, Teresa Silva, and everyone who shared their stories, for your help with this project.

Last, but most importantly, a very special "I love you" to my daughter, Beatrice, and my husband, Michael.

Foreword

Quilts are messengers and medicine. Both making and receiving them can be profound experiences. They link people together, whether they are friends and family, fellow guild members, or total strangers who have been warmed or inspired by a quilt that comes into their lives.

Victoria Findlay Wolfe understands all of this. She has quilting in her Minnesota farm girl blood, but it was as a budding painter in New York City that quilting began to gradually take over her life. As a new mother in the city, she discovered that quilts could be her primary medium of expression and source of income as well as her philanthropic focus and a centerpiece of her social life.

In *The Quilting Experience*, she has produced a truly remarkable book that invites the reader to ponder all the special connections and touchstones that quilts uniquely provide. Her personal stories are powerful and deftly told, and she begins each chapter by sharing her own experience. Then she offers a prompt that will summon the reader's responses to these themes. But the deep magic of this book is the myriad of other voices and stories she has collected and curated, so that the anecdotes of lives deepened by quilts and quilting pile up and interact. Whether reading a chapter focused on "Identity" or "Travel" or "Comfort and Healing" or "Traditions," the reader will feast on a wide range of evocative stories. Expect goose bumps and keep some tissues handy.

This poignant collection of personal stories would be something worth savoring and saving even if it didn't also operate as a pattern book. Impassioned teacher that she is, Victoria has created a quilt block tied to each chapter, and they can all be sewn together into what she calls a "kitchen sink" quilt. I can see individual quilters digging into this book with gusto and being inspired by the traditions and design ideas on their own. But there is a whole other level of opportunity presented: clearly, Victoria also would love to see guilds and groups use this volume creatively together.

My relationship with Victoria goes back several decades. I've known her as an interview subject (I interviewed Victoria for the Quilt Alliance project Quilters' Save Our Stories [QSOS] and for a profile in *QuiltCon* magazine in 2020); as a fellow board advisor for two vital quilt nonprofits; as a fellow member of an art quilt guild in Manhattan; and as an inspiration for my own quilting through her books and social media posts. Above all, I've had the privilege to know Victoria as a friend. I will never forget that she walked up to me at my husband's memorial service in 2015 with a quilt in her arms for my comfort.

I believe Victoria chose me to write a foreword for this book because in addition to being a passionate quilter myself, I've spent a lot of my journalistic years researching the significance and the mechanics of rituals and celebrations. I've written four books on tradition and only one on quilting, and my most popular lecture, Making Meaning, is all about how brilliant quilters are at celebrating life, and how they can amplify those instincts. This treasury of personal essays delighted me and unleashed memories of how these themes have played out in my own quilt life. I learned to quilt from my mother, and Victoria sparked a memory of finishing the last quilt my mother was working on when she died, so it could go to its intended recipient, my niece. And I remember that when I made myself a memorial quilt from my late husband's shirts and decided to fly without a pattern, to go the improv route, I used Victoria's 2012 book *15 Minutes of Play* to get me started. That's the quilt I would grab first if my house were on fire.

I think this book will spark even deeper and more soul-filling quilt experiences going forward in my life. And I believe it will do the same for you.

MEG COX
Princeton, New Jersey

Meg Cox is a journalist and book author.
A writer for the *Wall Street Journal* for 17 years, she now is a thought leader on the topics of quilting and family traditions. megcox.com

Introduction

My thoughts often drift to the past—the place I grew up, my grandmother's quilts, and the experiences that have shaped my life. As I work on my quilts, I'm constantly seeking connections between my past and present, and looking for inspiration in the moments that have defined me.

For me, quilting is the art of storytelling. Each quilt is a canvas for personal stories and emotions, reflecting the ebbs and flows of life. I craft quilts that hold memories and moments, mending my soul or lifting me up when I need it most.

In each of my books, I've explored techniques that shape my quilt-making process. These range from the power of play, which unlocks open-mindedness and enables free-form work, to drawing inspiration from the stories and memories that make up our lives, as well as mastering the technical skills that guarantee success. Perhaps most significantly, I encourage quilters to reflect on their own progress and recognize just how far they've come. It's my belief that each quilter possesses a unique tale to tell, and every quilt we create is a singular expression of our life experiences.

As we quilt, we can be intentional about the stories we're telling—from the fabrics we choose to the techniques we

use. By embracing the moments of our lives and weaving them into our quilts, we can create pieces that are not only beautiful, but deeply meaningful as well.

As a trained painter, I initially struggled to find my own voice with fiber art when I shifted my focus to quilting. I drew inspiration from my grandmother's scrappy polyester quilts, which were pieced by hand. However, I wanted to use cottons and make the quilts in my own style. I started as my grandmother had, by using a sheet as a base and stitching scraps of fabric onto it, using my machine's fancy stitches. The process quickly became tedious and overwhelming, and I abandoned the project, storing it away in a drawer for many years.

Years later, I revisited the project with fresh eyes, pulling out the leftover quilt blocks I had accumulated over time. I laid them out on my design wall, much like I would move around paint on a canvas, and began to see how I could piece them together to create a unique quilt that paid homage to my grandmother's work but also reflected my own style and vision.

I used everything at my disposal—fabrics I had collected over the years, scraps from other projects, the embroidery out of a kitchen towel—and I even cut up my own unfinished quilt tops to complete that quilt. I called it my "Everything but the Kitchen Sink" quilt, and it became a reflection of my life from 2000 to 2009. It held nine years of learning different quilt block techniques, as well as the moments that had defined me—from the passing of my grandmother to my marriage, the adoption of my daughter, and the new creative direction I was taking.

That quilt is not just about the designs or how visually appealing it is. It represents the rough and complicated aspects of life—its beauty and terror—and is the most important quilt I have ever made. It embodies a change in my creative process, my life's journey, the emotions of loss and rebirth, and every moment of my life is stitched into its fabric.

The process of creating that quilt is anything but conventional. Rather than following a set plan or cohesive design, each block represents a unique moment and stands on its own. The whole quilt tells a story of personal experiences, emotions, and memories, with each patch serving as a colorful reminder of a particular time in my life.

Over the years, I have created a multitude of these "kitchen sink" sampler quilts similar to this one, a unique tapestry of memories pieced together with fragments of finished or unfinished quilt parts that need a permanent home. With each new project, I delight in the process of arranging, adding, and discarding blocks, savoring each moment as I construct a narrative that flows across the quilt. It's a thrill to navigate the challenge of making seemingly random blocks complement one another, a game of creative Tetris that keeps me engaged and invested in the art of quilting.

Everything but the Kitchen Sink by Victoria Findlay Wolfe, quilted by Linda Sekerak, 2009, 89" × 93"

Introduction

I wanted to share with you a way to make your own "kitchen sink"–style quilt filled with your own experiences; this book is the vehicle to do so. I've chosen 12 themes to reflect on and consider, and for each theme I've designed a corresponding quilt block of various sizes to make up this Experience Quilt (page 22).

In each chapter, you'll find block instructions for that theme, and the amount and size of those blocks needed for the Experience Quilt. Some of the blocks have multiple sizes to add more variety in the quilt design, so the blocks fit together without having a typical grid layout. Speaking of fitting it all together, that involves making additional parts from some of the blocks to fill in the spaces, where needed. These "extra bits" will also be listed with the block instructions. However, I recommend that you wait until the end to make the extras and borders, since they are a great place to add in specific colors you might need to make all the blocks work well together. (See "The Experience Quilt Construction," page 190.)

EXPERIENCES

Quilting has brought immense gratitude into my life in so many ways. When I tell people that I am a professional quilt artist, I often hear one of two responses: "Oh, my grandmother makes quilts," or "You don't look like a quilter." I relish these moments because they give me the chance to hear their stories and show them that quilts are an art form and that we quilters come in all shapes, sizes, and styles, just like our quilts!

The friendships I have made through quilting have enriched my life and made my world a better place, and there have been so many from all over the world! Finding the threaded connection is not always "about a quilt" per se; it can happen in unexpected ways . . . I was flying back from the Houston International Quilt Festival when I first met one of my closest friends, Chris. He is a talented dancer and choreographer, and though he's not a quilter, he had a question about textiles, and I had sources to help him find what he needed for the stage. That day, we couldn't stop talking once we started. Five years later, our conversations continue, often about each other's creative processes, finding similarities and differences and embracing our art forms. Discovering commonalities between various artistic mediums is truly exciting to me because it opens unexpected connections and bridges between artists. He and I are now working on a collaborative piece together, and it's exciting to blend our processes into one work of art! This connection happened because of textiles! Simply amazing!

In one of our discussions about this book, Chris mentioned to me how in his sophomore year, a school trip brought them to Washington, DC, to see the AIDS Memorial quilts when they covered the entire National Mall, and what that moment meant for him. I love that we all can find moments where quilts have touched our lives. I can tell you now, that was the best time I ever had sitting in a middle seat on an airplane!

Had it not been for my childhood experiences with my grandmother's quilts and an environment full of creative outlets, I might not have had the privilege of meeting such beautiful souls or embarking on a journey deep into the world of quilting.

I thought, why not ask others to contribute their stories as well? We can all relate to these threaded tales and life experiences! So besides my musings, you will find stories from many different people, both quilters and nonquilters, who have had precious moments where quilts connect them in some way to their lives.

Another interesting experience I had was receiving a cold call from Amy Milne in 2011. As the executive director of the Quilt Alliance, she was searching for event spaces in New York City to host a fundraiser called Quilters Take Manhattan. After finding me through an online search for quilters in New York City, she thought I might be able to offer some advice. As it turned out, my spacious loft was perfect for hosting events, and my Empire Quilt Guild often held shows at the Fashion Institute of Technology, so I was able to pass this info along to her.

During our conversation, Amy explained that the Quilt Alliance's mission was to document, preserve, and share stories of quilts and quilters. We discussed the importance of labeling quilts and the organization's QSOS interviews (Quilters' Save Our Stories). Amy asked if they could interview me in my home as part of the Quilters Take Manhattan event they were planning. Though I was incredibly nervous to be in front of 100 people, I agreed. This was my very first interview about my work, just before my book *15 Minutes of Play* was released. The "touchstone" object I talked about was my "Everything but the Kitchen Sink" quilt (page 11). It is an interesting read for me to look back on and note how far I've come! You can read my QSOS interview by Meg Cox at www.qsos.quiltalliance.org/items/show/2222.

Receiving that one phone call resonated deeply with me, especially the importance of labeling our quilts and preserving our quilting heritage. As a result, I was invited to join the board of the Quilt Alliance and have since contributed to documenting stories through the NYC Metro Mod quilt guild, of which I was a founder. The beauty of the Quilt Alliance is that it's an opportunity for anyone to document their work. (See more on page 227.)

I invite you to explore the archives of the Quilt Alliance with its treasure trove of insights and experiences that are connected to specific quilts and quilters of all levels. It is crucial to label and claim ownership of one's work. Just imagine all the quilts we find with unknown makers, about which we know nothing, and the stories we wish we knew.

This book contains small snippets from numerous longer interviews that highlight the themes I have presented. When you see a QSOS story snippet within these pages, the full interview link is listed, along with the interviewer and the date of the recording. These interviews are transcribed from the actual interview.

Here is an example:

Q: What questions should we be asking about quilts and quiltmakers today, what questions should historians be asking?

Wow! Let me approach it this way: when I appraise quilts, somebody brings me an antique quilt and I look at this, the first thing we say is "If we could only know the story." And my very favorite quilts are sort of the kind that I make—the ones that make people scratch their heads and say, "Why did she do that?" And if there was some way to go back and find these really wild, crazy things and say, "What made her do that?" I'm all for good workmanship but I'm bored with it. When I see a quilt that shows me the soul of the maker, I get really, really excited. Or this woman says, "I am different and I was here," or "I didn't want to follow the rules and I was here." I think if we could really find the stories behind the quilts that's the main thing.

Teddy Pruett

interviewed by Amy Henderson for the Quilt Alliance's Quilters' Save Our Stories (QSOS) project, October 13, 2001
www.qsos.quiltalliance.org/items/show/2446

Planning

Over the past few years, I've found myself in a reflective state, contemplating my priorities and what's next on my journey. As I look toward the future, I'm drawn to the moments that bring us together—sharing stories, laughter, and the simple joy of creating something beautiful with our hands, refreshing my thoughts on being mindful of life. I like my quilts to have a story. I like harnessing the energy that was happening within me while I was creating.

These moments have often centered on quilting. There's something special about gathering with friends over a meal and stitching together, letting conversations unfold organically as we connect. Also, as I reflect on my past 12 years of teaching and travel, it's the conversations with students that have meant the most to me—the stories shared and the bonds made as we find similarities in our lives. These are threads of life I embed in my work.

Through this project, I encourage you to share your stories and recognize the ways that quilting is a gift in your life. We often hold quilts in our hands from unknown makers and wonder what was happening in the quilter's life. Why did they make the choices they did? What were they thinking while adding all those tiny stitches?

I invite you to consciously find your own life threads to add to your work. What is happening in your life that is subconsciously leading your color choices? Or the choice in pattern, complex or easy, depending on what emotional layers you carry today.

As you read through my theme prompts, make note of the memories that float up for you. As you continue to read the stories submitted by others, find ways to relate your own life, touching on any and all the emotions. Yes, we can easily relate quilts to a sad memory, but when we gather together with our quilt friends, we often do so to laugh! Make sure to remember the happy, joyful, exciting times, along with the poignant heartstring moments.

Quilting brings amazing experiences and connections into your creative space, and with each new stitch, there's the potential for something truly magical to unfold.

The Experience Quilt is a project for you to make and reflect on the journey and to ponder, while creating, the ways in which quilts have touched your life. Through this book, there are a few different ways you might want to approach it: individually, through a quilting bee, or within a group.

Individually:

Reading my prompts at the beginning of each chapter and then diving into the stories from others, work your way through the book one chapter at a time. Perhaps grab a notebook, and journal your own stories that correlate with the themes mentioned. Sometimes your stories are about a quilt, or perhaps while you were at a quilt event an unexpected encounter happened. I invite you to ponder your own life experiences while you construct your blocks. Add your stories to your quilt; select fabrics and colors that help tell the story.

As a Quilting Bee:

A newer definition of "a quilting bee" is a social event to make and contribute quilt blocks for each other in order to complete a quilt with many hands/help.

Gather a group of 11 friends (or family members!—plus you to make 12) and assign each one a chapter. Allow them to make the blocks according to their own experiences and choices. Each can make the assigned blocks and give them back to you to make a quilt that reflects everyone's journey.

You could also repeat this for all 11 members, so everyone eventually ends up with their own quilt.

I invited 11 friends and assigned them each their block. I asked them to use whatever colors they wanted, but not to use brown or solids. I was the twelfth member. I then arranged all the *completely random blocks*, and I finished by adding in what I thought pulled them all together visually for my blocks and the extra bits. (See the Friends Experience Quilt on page 26.)

Planning

Within a Group:

By working on your own blocks within a weekly/monthly group who are also working on their own blocks, you can then share your stories/memories/anecdotes and your blocks you made for a group discussion.

Like a book club, sewing bee, and show-and-tell all in one! (Make sure there are cake, cookies, and coffee too, if it's an in-person event! Or if your friends are far away, make it a Zoom party so you can share the powerful conversations that come up, and stay connected to your pals!)

COLOR

Besides working through this book individually or with a group, you have some opportunities to approach *color* in a few ways as well.

You can follow the suggested themes and create the required blocks, staying close to the colors I have chosen in the Experience Quilt.

You will notice in the first three blocks that you will make, all my blocks have a variety of red in certain positions. If you have a favorite color, say, blue . . . then blue can land in the red positions to get a similar effect for your final outcome.

OR:

Let the quilt evolve organically and take on a life of its own by each time selecting fabrics that make you happy!

Embrace your own creativity and consciously choose fabrics and colors that reflect your current mood or emotional state. By letting go of any preconceived notions about color and pattern, you open yourself up to a world of possibilities and allow your intuition to guide you to the perfect fabric for each block. Let life dictate what the outcome of your quilt will look like. That kind of risk-taking provides a multitude of lessons, and you will make a very thoughtful quilt.

OR:

Challenge your own process.

I spend a lot of time identifying the parts of my process that I tend to do over and over, and I look for ways to change it up and try to make a quilt unlike anything I've made before. By doing so, you too can make purposeful choices based on identifying the palette of colors you always use and finding a way to break your routine. Always make scrappy quilts? Try to make this in a two-color quilt, or limited palette, say, red and white or a single color / dark background (like the Family Experience Quilt on page 25). What colors might you choose?

OR:

Throw all caution to the wind and see what happens when you let loose of the constraints!

As an example, in my Friends Experience Quilt (page 26), once I received the blocks back from my 11 players, it was my turn to look at all the blocks and determine what these last blocks needed to be to make the quilt balance. Since my chapter was 12, which are the Bunting blocks and borders, the Bunting blocks allowed me to add in a variety of colors that helped tie the quilt together. I then focused on what was happening in the middle of the quilt, to help determine what my borders should be. The blocks as a whole are very warm toned, with a smattering of dark blocks. The four large Bear Paw Heart blocks were pinks and oranges, with dark blues. Those colors are what I used to make my scrappy borders.

A few good rules to balance a quilt:

- Pick bold colors from your center area and repeat it out at the borders—an easy and effective way to balance your quilt. See how that relates to each of the three examples shown on pages 22, 25, and 26.

- Find your lightest value and darkest value. If your quilt is looking muddy, the lightest value and darkest value should be added to help push the foreground and backgrounds visually. This also means that all colors can of course live happily together by following a variety of value choices. Light does not necessarily mean white . . . dark does not mean black. Squint at your quilt blocks: Which colors stand out as light or dark? Everything else is a medium.

- Play with placement of the blocks you made within the layout. Each block is used multiple times, so you are able to sort the blocks you made to evenly scatter your color values around the quilt . . . this helps with a cohesive flow around your quilt. If, at the end, you need to make an extra block or two, it's totally okay. I prefer to use what I made, though, because those are the pieces I made with purpose and intent, and they represent those moments in my life that day. I rarely exclude anything from my quilts when I'm working on them. I find a way to make it work.

Planning

The Experience Quilt by Victoria Findlay Wolfe, quilted by Shelly Pagliai, 2023

FABRIC

As with most scrappy quilts, individual yardage requirements can be difficult to determine, and the beauty is often in the repetition or substitution of similar fabrics. So these requirements are written **only as a guide** to get you started in the right direction.

Background color (*white fabrics*)	assorted pieces to total 5½ yards
Feature fabrics	½ yard each of 3 fabrics (*solid red, solid dark red, navy*) ¼ yard each of 24 fabrics (*used in larger blocks or in multiple blocks*) Variety of 6" × 6" scraps—⅛ yard pieces from approx. 44 fabrics
Borders	1¼ yard background fabric (*white print*) ½ yard feature fabric (*solid dark red*)
Binding	¾ yard
Fabric for backing	8½ yards
Batting	102" × 102"

CUTTING AND PRESSING MATTERS

Templates, where needed, for the blocks are in the back of the book.

All templates and cutting measurements include ¼" seam allowance.

When cutting directional pieces (right and left/reverse shapes) from templates, fold fabric in half and cut around one template through the two layers. This gives you both directions at once.

Most of the time I'm pressing to one side in this quilt. I will tell you that it's not always a straight-forward answer though, and I want to share with you tips for making a good judgment call that will be helpful on this quilt, *and* for many other quilting projects in general.

Planning

1. Pressing to the darker fabric.

    A good classic tidbit of knowledge if you are sewing with a light background choice.

2. Pressing away from multiple seams.

    This will generally keep the thickness of the quilt top more even, avoiding spots where the seam allowances pile up. Sometimes, pressing a fabric one way is an opportunity to then flip it over and *look* at it and see if it behaved properly. At these moments, sometimes pressing these seams open is best, or not . . . look at it; how does it look from the front?

3. Pressing seams open to make your points appear.

    Sometimes we know we *nailed* our points perfectly, but then we press the fabric to one side and look at it, and the point is not there. Try pressing that seam open; your point may appear. If not, remember, it is your call if you want to fix your point. If you've sewn it *off*, it's *not* magically going to appear. If you need/want to fix a point, remember not to rip the whole block off . . . just open your seam a ½", re-pin your point, and re-sew just that point.

This book is more than just a collection of quilt patterns. It's an invitation to be mindful and intentional in our creative pursuits, and to reflect on the role that quilting has played in our lives.

As you work through the blocks and themes in this book, take time to consider why you create and what inspires you. Think about the ways that quilting has had an impact on your life, and how it has touched the lives of others. Reflect on the rich history and traditions of quilting and the ways that those who came before us used this art form to tell their own stories and create connections across time and space.

Through this book and your own creative process, you have the power to make something beautiful and meaningful. Be conscious of the life around you and create with intention and purpose.

Consider the challenges and triumphs of those who have faced similar experiences in different eras, and honor their legacies with gratitude and pride. By doing so, you can connect with others, honor the past, and create something truly special that will inspire and uplift for generations to come.

Each block in this book has been thoughtfully designed to serve as a stepping-stone toward telling your story. By following the suggested themes and creating the required blocks, you'll gain the skills and confidence needed to branch out and experiment with your own fabric choices, color palettes, and design ideas.

As you work on the blocks, some may come easily to you while others may present a learning curve. But rest assured that none of these blocks are so difficult that you won't be able to enjoy the process. Embrace partial seam construction! Partial seams are *not* difficult (see my *Modern Quilt Magic* book

Family Experience Quilt by Elaine Howard, Jean Howard, Katie Howard, Lauren Howard, Willow Howard, Kim Hryniewicz, Erin Keeven, Lucy Keeven, Fiona Scheer, Jessica Scheer, Rhys Scheer, Patti Scheer, Susan Scheer, Beth Snyder, and Amelia Snyder, quilted by Kim Hryniewicz, 2023

Friends Experience Quilt by Melanie Anderson, Jade Benjamin, Kelsey Danley, Victoria Findlay Wolfe, Kim Hryniewicz, Deb Hunter, Tony Jacobson, Edie McGinnis Shelly Pagliai, Kate Pietschman, Lolly Schiffman, and Jan Wisor, quilted by Julie Hirt, 2023

for more on partial seams!). A partial seam is a straight seam you start and stop before the end, coming back later to finish sewing it. (Not hard at all, it provides you another method for your quilt construction!)

In my years of teaching, I've found that when we need to learn something new, it often takes six to eight attempts before we find our groove. This is perfectly normal, and it's important to give yourself grace and space to make mistakes and learn from them. After all, if you don't make mistakes, you don't learn anything!

You will find at the back of this book more ways the blocks used individually (or paired with another) can create beautiful and unique designs that will help you continue to tell your own quilt story. Individually, all the blocks come together to form a cohesive design. Or play with mixing two or more blocks for a fun, unexpected outcome.

The blocks of the Experience Quilt are of various sizes that mathematically can be arranged for your own quilt layout as well! (See page 197.)

Please take your time, enjoy the process, and let your creativity guide you as you embark on this quilting journey.

Remember that the goal of quilting is not perfection, but rather progress and growth. Each mistake is an opportunity to learn and improve your skills. And above all, remember that you are precious, and the fabric is just fabric—you have more! Don't be afraid to cut it up and experiment! Last, and most importantly, enjoy every stitch.

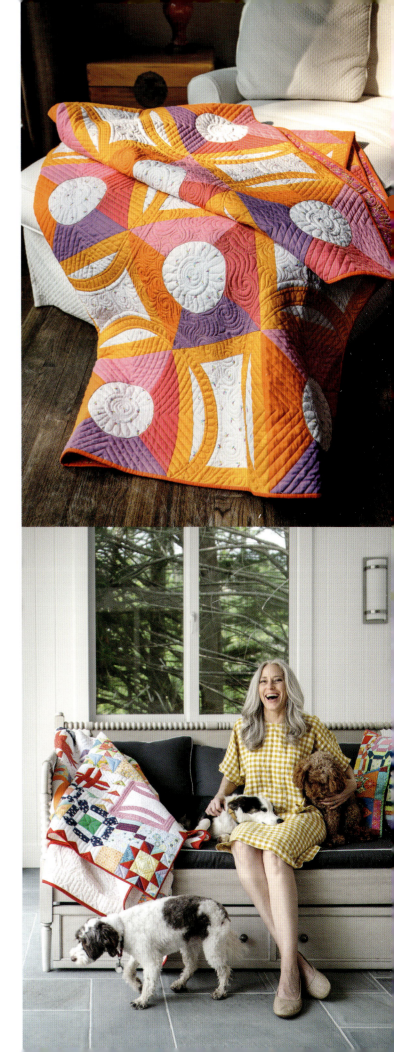

CHAPTER 1

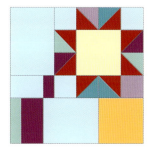

Identity

As the granddaughter of a quilter and a child who learned various creative skills such as quilting, embroidery, painting, drawing, and woodwork, I always knew I wanted to grow up to be an artist. I have, over the years, wrestled with where I came from and where I am now, and I've used my quilt making to help answer those questions. Yes, I'm an artist; I love all different forms of making. So am I a quilter? A painter? Or a universal maker?

I find that keeping that question a curiosity and open ended lets me continue to push my own intuition to search for the answer, which helps me generate more and more ideas. In this way, I find that improvisational thinking is applied to everything that I do, the way I think, make choices, and create. I refuse to be boxed into one format of style, type, or label, and that curious behavior also keeps me engaged in my playful practices.

When I was a child and making quilts, I was selecting fabrics I thought were pretty from my mother's stash of fabrics. When I started making quilts for myself, I often chose solids because I had a "Quilts of Lancaster Country" poster that hung in my bedroom. I made those choices by looking at what was around me, but who am I as a quilter and a creative person? Is quilting a part of my identity? If so, how?

When my daughter was young, and I was known mainly as "Beatrice's Mom," I was selecting fabrics that I knew she would love. I picked happy colors of the rainbow because "rainbow" was her favorite color until she turned five and woke up saying her favorite color was brown. But that's a different story. I had so much fun making her quilts, one after the other, until she found one she wanted to cuddle with!

Around that time, I recall connecting with quilter Kathie Holland through my blog. She asked for a bag of scraps since I had mentioned I was being overrun by the rainbow scraps from all these

quilts. I sent her a bagful, which she promptly started making into the cutest tiny tumblers. When I saw what she had made with my scraps, I got all choked up. Those were my daughter's scraps! How attached I was to those adorable little scraps! Apparently, it came across loud and clear, since Kathie very generously sent me the quilt top and I finished it into a quilt and have put it aside for my daughter to have. I was so emotionally invested in those precious bits of fabric; it was a big eye-opener for me! I was surprised at the feelings that came up in seeing the fabrics I had selected in someone else's quilt.

I always found it easier to select fabrics to make quilts for other people or to select fabrics for telling a particular story. But when it came time to make a quilt for my own bed, I selected browns, purples, hot pinks, and navy blues, not colors that people may think of when looking at my work in general. To me, these are nesting colors. I want warm, enveloping colors around me. Making those choices for myself and what I wanted in my living space pushed me to explore colors I don't normally create with, but when I'm creating to tell a story, I need all colors to be invited to the party!

When it comes to fabric, the colors I choose, patterns I make, and so on show a part of my identity as a quilt maker. I often hear people say, "I knew that was your quilt before I saw your name." To me, that's funny to hear, because my goal when making a new project is to try to make a quilt that doesn't look like I made it—that looks different from my others! The reality is that the core of who I am will always visually show up in the works that I create.

The act of creation is a vital force in my life, one that gives me purpose and a sense of wholeness. Without the constant flow of ideas and inspiration, I feel lost and incomplete. This realization has brought me to a profound understanding of myself—that I am at my best when I am busy with the creative process. While the medium I work with may shift and evolve, my passion for creating never wanes. Currently, my obsession lies in the intricate art of quilt making, a pursuit that has become a vital part of my identity.

There is something indescribably fulfilling about the process of cutting and manipulating fabric to form something both visually stunning and practical. Each stitch tells a story, and each thread traces a piece of my soul woven into something beautiful, functional, and deeply personal.

IDENTITY: Spirited Star Block

FOR THE 12" BLOCK:

Star points *solid red*

4 squares 2⅞" × 2⅞", cut in half diagonally (8 triangles)

Star Center *yellow print*

1 square 4½" × 4½"

Corner Square *orange print*

1 square 4½" × 4½"

Star Trail *burgundy print*

1 square 2⅞" × 2⅞", cut in half diagonally (2 triangles)

1 (C) rectangle 1½" × 2½"

1 (E) rectangle 2½" × 4½"

Background *light print*

3 squares 2½" × 2½"

1 (A) rectangle 4½" × 6½"

1 (B) rectangle 3½" × 2½"

1 (F) rectangle 5½" × 4½"

Background Accent I *solid aqua*

1 square 2⅞" × 2⅞", cut in half diagonally (2 triangles)

1 (D) rectangle 1½" × 4½"

Background Accent II *solid lavender*

1 square 2⅞" × 2⅞", cut in half diagonally (1 triangle needed)

1 square 2½" × 2½"

Background Accent III *teal print*

2 squares 2⅞" × 2⅞", cut in half diagonally (3 triangles needed)

Half-Square Triangles

1. Sew each of the burgundy, aqua, lavender, and teal triangles to a red triangle to form half-square triangles (HSTs). Press seam allowances toward the red triangle. Trim the dog-ears at the corners.

Star Unit

1. Arrange the light print and lavender small squares, HSTs, and yellow star center square as shown.

2. Sew the HSTs together in pairs, pinning to match the diagonal seams. Press the seam to one side and check that the "inner points" of the star are ¼" from the raw edge. If they aren't, fix these seams now before proceeding.

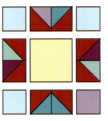

3. Sew the star together in rows, pressing each seam allowance toward the square.

4. Pinning at the intersecting seams, sew rows together to create star block, and press seam allowances in one direction.

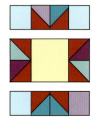 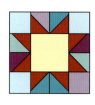

Side Rectangle Unit

1. Lay out (A), (B), and (C) rectangles as shown. Sew (B) and (C) together.

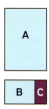

2. Sew this pieced rectangle to bottom of the (A) rectangle. Press seam toward (A).

3. Sew the side rectangle to the left side of the star block.

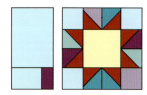

Bottom Rectangle Unit

1. Lay out (D) rectangle, (E) rectangle, (F) rectangle, and the orange print corner square as shown. Sew together. Press seams in the opposite direction of the seams in the rest of the block, so seam allowances will nest when sewn together.

2. Sew bottom pieced row to the star block row to complete block. Block measures 12½" × 12½".

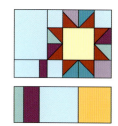 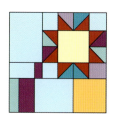

BLOCKS NEEDED FOR EXPERIENCE QUILT

12" Spirited Star blocks *(quilt corners) make 4 blocks*

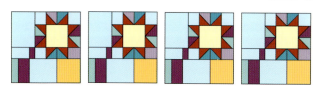

EXTRA BITS NEEDED FOR EXPERIENCE QUILT

As noted on p. 13, you may want to wait to make the Extra Bits until the end, after all the blocks are completed and arranged.

Star Units *make 2*

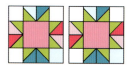

Half-Square Triangles *make 6*

Long Strip from middle of block: B, C, 2 squares (2½" × 2½"), and 2 HSTs *make 2*

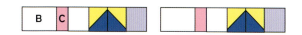

2½" squares *cut 4*

Identity

Threads of Identity

A SEWING ROOM OF ONE'S OWN

Long before I was aware that women must have a "room of one's own" to create art of their own, I learned this lesson from my grandmother. This story is about what she taught me, in her own room, about herself, about quilting, and about the need for a refuge, a haven—a room in which creativity flourishes. It is also about recognizing my own need for a sewing room of my own—a need I know I share with so many others.

My grandmother Kate Dunham created her own private sewing "room" in a corner of her cellar. With walls made of quilts, she carved off a space between the coal chute and the octopus arms of the furnace, where she kept her sewing machine (a '52 Singer), quilt frames, and a straight-back kitchen chair. It was her private space in the Toronto home where she'd raised six children as a single mother, widowed on the cusp of the Great Depression. By the time I arrived on the scene, the family knew to leave my grandmother to her own devices when she was in her sewing room. But I was fortunate to be invited in. She knew I was interested in learning to quilt. Before I sat quilting with her, she'd sit me underneath the quilt frames, where I'd pass her the needles she'd dropped. And, I listened and learned.

Quilting was my grandmother's passion. I'm convinced she used it to save herself. It gave her worth (she was keeping her family warm during cold Canadian winters) and provided an outlet for her creative energy. Her sewing room was where she could be most herself, where she could escape the demands of motherhood, of supporting her family, of fending off bill collectors, of figuring out how she'd get through her days. In her quiet, safe space, quilting was nourishing and contemplative. She recognized that this room was a basic need for her.

My sewing room is aboveground, in a vacated spare bedroom. It's not fancy, fitted out with furniture drawn from other corners of the house. But the best part—apart from it belonging to me alone—is the sewing machine. It's my grandmother's Singer. Perfect for quilting and a perfect reminder of her.

In her iconic 1929 essay "A Room of One's Own," Virginia Woolf called for the histories of the anonymous women whose stories have never been told. My grandmother is one of those anonymous women. She could so easily slip from view, having lived a quiet, unobtrusive, unacknowledged life. This story is a way of ensuring her legacy lives.

That's the power of story. I know Kate Dunham was in no way unique. Her story is that of thousands like her, who found their own rooms and made hundreds of quilts. If we're lucky, we still have a few of those quilts on our beds, and we still share the stories and the names of the women who made them.

Susan Lightstone

EARLY DISCOVERY

When I was 11 years old, I was trying to find my passion. That may seem a little early for someone to find their passion, but it's worked out fine for me.

My sisters are amazing at painting and drawing, So I thought that maybe I'd enjoy that. I sat down at the kitchen table and tried drawing some people. About 45 minutes into it, my mom looked over my shoulder and asked how it was going. I told her that I was frustrated and that it looked bad, and she asked, "Are you enjoying doing it?," to which I responded, "No, I hate it!"

My mom told me that if we're going to spend free time doing something, it might as well be something that we love. That was my lesson that I am not an artist like my sisters, and I started trying to find what I love.

A few weeks later I was in our activity room, and I noticed some fabric on a shelf. My first project was a very haphazard four-patch pillow. My mom still remembers me running up the stairs with the pillow and telling her, "Mom, I found what I love!"

We went to the local quilt shop in town, and countless ladies there taught me so much about sewing, and life in general. I learned that "old ladies" can be a pretty fun bunch, and now the majority of my friends are at least 20 years older than me.

As soon as I turned 14, the quilt shop put me on the payroll, and when I moved to a different town, I eventually found my way to another quilt shop, where I've been working for about a year and a half now.

It's been eight years since I started sewing; I can still be found in my sewing room almost every day, doing what I love and trying to make the world a more colorful place.
Happy sewing!

Jade Benjamin

DIVA SEWING

I was working on a quilt project with a group of friends, using the book *Beyond the Block*. Our challenge rules included using components from the book and something from a Lorelei Sewing Diva fabric, a quirky, fun novelty print with women in different outfits. I chose a diva that represented me the best, then decided she needed a ring in her navel.

When I told my husband I needed to shop for a belly button ring, he paused and then he told me I should think about it before I did anything like that. He actually thought I was looking for a ring for my navel in my 75-year-old body! I made the quilt, and everyone still laughs at the story.

Ruth Paul

Q: How would you say quiltmaking is an important part of your life?

It's part of my identity, I think. I have always sewn. When I was growing up, and I was sewing clothes and my sisters were sewing clothes. I used to get such a charge out of making something no one else had—to be unique; I loved to sew. I would get so excited. One of the things I've learned as I got older was patience. I'm getting better at it, being patient, not so great all the time, but striving to slow down. When I was a kid, I didn't have any patience, and I just rushed through things, and thus my garments were not made very well. I have always been drawn to bright colors. I would go, and I would pick out the most bright, colorful, crazy, garish patterns that I could possibly find, and I made my clothes. I was so proud. As I got older, my older sisters didn't sew as much. They looked at it as a chore, and they looked at it as drudgery or something that they had to do, and I've never felt that way. I've always looked at it as a possibility, and as a joy, and a way to express my emotions. If sometimes life gets really hard, I find that's when I make my best quilts because there's always a sense of hope and possibility. That's what I like about quilting and garment sewing. For me, it is a part of how I define myself. I can't imagine not creating something—to me, it's like breathing.

Andrea Brokenshire
interviewed by Sandi Goldman for the Quilt Alliance's Quilters' Save Our Stories (QSOS) project, November 5, 2011
www.qsos.quiltalliance.org/items/show/2422

Q: In what way do you think your quilts reflect the area where you live?

Well, let's see. I live in the San Francisco Bay Area, and we are ethnically very mixed, which my quilts are. My own guild is all different ages, incomes, and racial and ethnic backgrounds. San Francisco is very much a hodgepodge, and so are my quilts because I don't have just one style. I bounce around. [. . .] So from that standpoint, my quilts and who I am is very much reflected by where I live. In my area, people are open to whatever's out there. There's not one right way to do anything. And I think that's very much influenced me. I came to California when I was five from New York and had my education in California. As I compare and contrast to other parts of the United States or other countries, what I see is that I was brought up more with the notion of multiple choice. That is, there's more than one way to do things. And to go to other places and this is the way it has always been and it's the only way it will ever be, so that I think has broadened me.

I grew up in Southern California, and going to the San Francisco area was just mind exploding for me. There was a very strong Asian influence. At that point when I was in Los Angeles [there] was a very small Asian community. It's now very large down there, but not when I was growing up. Seeing all the Asian textiles and garments and artwork has influenced me a lot. Part of it with Japanese design is simplicity. In many of my quilts, there is a simplicity. They're not necessarily fancy quilts because I think simple is good enough. You don't have to be real complicated. That's someone else's job.

Roberta Horton
interviewed by Marilyn Geary for the Quilt Alliance's Quilters' Save Our Stories (QSOS) project, October 23, 1999
www.qsos.quiltalliance.org/items/show/2479

Q: *Tell me how you began.*

I was raised in a family of artists. My father was a painter, my mother was a sculptor, my older brother is a documentary filmmaker, my sister-in-law is a ceramic sculptor; the list just goes on. My daughter tends to call it the family curse. [*Laughs.*] I never intended to be an artist; you never want to do what your parents do. I planned to be a writer and then I became an institutional editor instead of a writer, but I was always interested in textile arts and I did them as a kind of semi-professional hobby. I was a weaver as a young woman, and I was part of a weaving cooperative where I sold jackets and things like that. Then I got married and had young children. There wasn't space for the loom and it got put away. When I was pregnant with my first child, a friend of mine asked me if I wanted to take a quilting class, which I did, and I found that I really liked it—although it took me ten years to finish my first piece! [*Laughs.*] My plan was always to be a utilitarian quilter; I was going to make bed quilts and pillowcases and that kind of stuff. I had no intention of doing anything for the wall. Gradually, the pieces became more and more intended as wall objects (even though they were still flat quilts) and I started to sort of skirt around the edges of the art quilt movement. It wasn't until I added some three-dimensional elements to a flat piece that any of the art quilting really took hold for me. It was as if once I had broken a major rule of quilting, which is that it is supposed to be flat, everything else was then up for grabs, and it has been like having a tiger by the tail ever since.

Susan Else
interviewed by Karen Musgrave for the Quilt Alliance's Quilters' Save Our Stories (QSOS) project, April 30, 2008
www.qsos.quiltalliance.org/items/show/2595

Q: *Why is quiltmaking important to you?*

Everybody has to express themselves in some kind of way, and there is a real tranquility that I get. Even though if you walked into my studio when I'm working and you see scraps on the floor and you see me leaning against the wall with a frown on my face, with the scissors held almost like a dagger, you wouldn't think that, but there is a real peace that I get from making quilts, whether they are traditional or wall hangings. I took ballet for ten years when I was growing up, and that was kind of my artistic outlet then, and I kind of miss it, having that, and so I think this also fills kind of the artistic need for me. Obviously, it's not for everybody, but for me, I think it does fill that, that I can express something. . . .

Q: How do you want to be remembered?

A question that I really haven't given any thought to. Let's see, I would like to be remembered as the crazy lady who brought the sewing machine to school once a year and let the children sew on it [*laughs*], because the kids love it. I also would like for people to just say, "She did really good work. I enjoy looking at the things she made." I'm a simple person, I don't need to be . . . I would love to win some awards, but that is not necessary. If I like it, then that is what I want people to say. She made stuff that she liked, and it made other people happy too . . .

Jackie Cambell
interviewed by Karen Musgrave for the Quilt Alliance's Quilters' Save Our Stories (QSOS) project, January 21, 2009
www.qsos.quiltalliance.org/items/show/2573

CONTENTMENT

I spent decades building, fostering, and prioritizing my career. Throughout advanced education, weekly business travel, leading and supporting teams, and providing solutions for customers, I aimed to serve up what was next asked of me. Though that was rewarding and productive in providing for my family, my inner heart did not quite feel connected to the present. I was quietly seeking contentment. Unexpectedly, I found it at my first quilt retreat.

Yes, I learned to create design with *new* eyes, *new* tools, and *new* techniques. Cut it up! It's only fabric! Move those pieces around on the design wall! Watch how your eyes move across the design! I learned all those creative processes to really expand my quilting repertoire. But what I did not expect was the transformation of *identity*. The explosive change to my inner self—how I gave permission to see myself, let go, cry a few tears, and embrace the change that was taking place. I learned to open my heart to be comfortable with exploring the unknown. My quilt started with a vision and a pile of fabric. I thought I had a plan for the design, but then I began to play with the colors, or their placement, and the design shifted. I gave myself permission to be fearless in creating. And in this process, a truth was revealed. I could be content in the present moment, void of fear, absent of doubt, and lacking any shame. As I was embracing risks, creating parts and building a design, my heart was also letting go. Letting go of the self that was always present for others and just being present to myself. I was giving myself permission to surround myself with creative cohorts and not feel weakened by domineering voices of my daily work life. The self-discovery was profound . . . a few tears for the years I spent searching, gratitude to reconnect with the spirit of quilting in my late Grandma Angela Emge and Great-Grandma Clara Wicklein, appreciation that I could create something that holds meaning, and revelation of the truth that I experience my deepest inner peace and flow while creating.

I discovered I am where I need to be, and I am learning what I need to learn in this very moment. The essence of contentment. And the quilt that I started at this retreat, I named "Contentment." My identity shifted that day. *I am a quilter.*

Carol Wesolik

Q: Do you feel pretty welcomed within the quilt community?

Yes, I have been. I won't even say it is a novelty thing like, "Oh look, a man, a quilter." I think it's just as a rule, quilters have a more openness about them and are a little more welcoming. And if someone comes along who's doing some quilting who has something different to show them, they will say, "Hey, look at that! Let's go along with that." I don't think people are looking at me as "Oh, my Lord, he's a man and he quilts." Or, "Oh, my Lord, he's black and he quilts." It's simply "Oh, he quilts."

[. . .] Of course, I'm not a typical quilter for the obvious reasons, male and black, but there's another aspect of me that when I tell quilters, there is an audible gasp. I admit that I do not have a stash of fabric. I will buy fabric and/or dye fabric for a specific project and do my best to use it up. Whatever I don't use up, I'll give it to my dad. (I talked about teaching him to sew. I also taught him to quilt.) [. . .]So I don't keep fabric on hand and whatever I'm using, I'm using. And once I've used it to the point where I think, "Alright, I'm tired of this. It needs to go out," I'll go buy something different for the next project and never have a room full of fabric.

There is the saying that "the one with the most fabric wins." Well, I'm assuming that is after you die, and I'm thinking, "Well, you know the one who dies with the most fabric is still dead, so what good did the fabric do?" I don't have a stash, I don't haunt quilt shops too much, and I don't buy the latest book and magazine and tool. I quilt because I enjoy quilting. I quilt because it is, as I said before, relaxing. It is very peaceful, and my quilts suit me.

I entered only one contest, and this was many years ago. It was a Snail's Trail quilt, and it wasn't a very big piece, but it was the best work I'd done to that day. (Of course, every quilt I make, I think, "This is the best one I've made.") Well, I entered that quilt in a contest, and it didn't win, and I was called and told, "Mr. Houston, you need to come and pick up your quilt on such and such a day." Okay, I went to pick up my quilt, and the place was full of other people whose quilts also did not win, and I realized we all had the same expression on our faces. We all expected our quilt to win, and at that point, I said, "You know what? I will not enter another contest because what's the point of being able to say my quilt is better than your quilt? Each and every quilt that gets made is a winning quilt."

I don't worry about the quilts being perfect. I'll sew because I'm happily sewing, and if I make a mistake, the mistake stays. I'm not going to rip out stitches [because I feel] they have to be perfect. I run into people who are very much into perfection, and I say, "Well, only God is perfect, and no, I don't think you fit the bill." I try to encourage people to let loose, cut loose, have fun, make your quilt and the only people that will know it's not perfect is you. Back when I was showing my early quilts to someone, they'd say "Oh, this is wonderful," and I'd say, "Well, yeah, but if you look in this little corner here you'll see that is not quite right, and if you look over there . . ." Most people didn't even notice what I noticed as being imperfections in the quilt. That is when I realized if they don't care, then neither do I.

Raymond Houston
interviewed by Karen Musgrave for the Quilt Alliance's Quilters' Save Our Stories (QSOS) project, August 20, 2008
www.qsos.quiltalliance.org/items/show/2610

CHAPTER 2

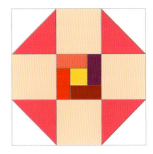

Traditions

Quilting traditions are deeply woven into the fabric of my life, both in terms of my personal history and my creative process. While I can trace my quilting lineage back to my grandmother, beyond that the trail goes cold. My daughter knows how to sew and has even made a few quilts, but whether or not she chooses to pursue it as a hobby remains to be seen. I'm happy to have passed on the vision and tradition of quilting to her, but I'm also excited to see where her own creativity takes her.

For me, quilting has always been a way to connect with my family's past and create something tangible and lasting out of the memories and stories of my youth. From the colorful patchwork quilts that my grandmother stitched together in the early 1960s to '80s, to the more contemporary designs that I've been experimenting with in the '80s until now. Each quilt I make tells a unique story about my family and my own creative journey.

But quilting traditions don't just stem from family ties. They also come from the larger quilting community that I've been lucky enough to be a part of. Whether it's attending a quilting bee, swapping blocks and scraps with fellow quilters online, or simply admiring the work of other quilters on social media, I'm constantly inspired by the creative energy and camaraderie that permeates the quilting world and adds to the traditions.

I've also been able to create my own traditions within the quilting world. From developing my own style and techniques to passing on my knowledge and passion to others, I feel like I'm contributing to the ever-evolving legacy of quilting.

Quilting is a craft that has been around for centuries in many different cultures, and as such, it has a rich history of traditions and techniques that have been passed down through generations. These traditions can manifest in a variety of ways, from the materials used to the patterns created, and even the social and cultural significance of quilting.

One way to categorize these traditions in quilting is the use of certain materials. For example, many quilters use cotton fabric for their quilts, since it is durable and easy to work with and can be found in a wide range of colors and prints. Additionally, some quilters prefer to use other fibers such as wool, silk, or crimplene, or recycling what is available for added texture and visual interest.

Another tradition in quilting is the use of certain patterns or designs. Quilting patterns have evolved over time, from simple geometric shapes to intricate and detailed designs. Some patterns and practices, such as the log cabin, the nine-patch, or using up every scrap, have been used for generations and are instantly recognizable as traditional quilting designs.

For me, quilting is not just about the materials and patterns; it is also a social and cultural tradition. I have been a part of quilting groups and guilds where I have connected with other quilters, shared my skills and knowledge, and felt a sense of community and support. I have also learned about the cultural significance of quilting, such as its use as a form of storytelling in African American history, as well as a way to preserve Indigenous cultural traditions.

These traditions are not just a part of the legacy I receive as a quilter; they also inspire me to continue pushing the boundaries of my creativity and exploring new techniques and materials. I see my quilts as a reflection of my own experiences and the traditions that have come before me, and I hope to pass on this legacy to future generations of quilters.

When I'm asked if my daughter quilts, I always enjoy sharing this story:

I received a call from Stevii Graves one day, and she asked if I was interested in making a quilt for her upcoming exhibition called *Personal App Quilts*. She explained that the quilt should represent who I am in the shape of an app on a phone. I immediately agreed and said, "Sure, I'd be glad to!"

Stevii then asked if I thought my daughter, Beatrice, would be interested in making a quilt as well. I hesitated and replied, "I doubt it. She always tells me that quilting is what I do, not what she does." Stevii encouraged me to ask Beatrice anyway, so I called out to her, "Hey, Beatrice, Stevii wants to know if you'll make a quilt for her exhibit."

Beatrice replied, "No thank you." I relayed her response to Stevii, and she quickly said, "Tell her the exhibit will travel all around the world." I repeated the message to Beatrice, and after a brief moment of contemplation, she said, "Okay, yeah, I'll make one!"

Even if my daughter is not currently interested in quilting, the fact that she agreed to participate in the exhibition shows that she has some appreciation for the art form and may be open to exploring it further in the future. Who knows, perhaps my hope for her to carry on the tradition is not as distant as it may appear!

What are ways in which traditions speak to you and your legacy?

TRADITIONS: Constant Classic Block

FOR THE 12" BLOCK:

Half-Square Triangles *red print & solid white*

 2 squares 4⅞" × 4⅞" each from 2 fabrics

Squares *orange print*

 4 squares 4½" × 4½"

Center Block Rectangles *4 different solid reds*

 1 rectangle 3¼" × 1¾" each from 4 red solids

Center Block Square *yellow print*

 1 square 2" × 2"

Half-Square Triangles

1. Mark a diagonal line on the backside of the two white half-square triangle squares from the upper left corner to the lower right corner.

2. Stack a red print and white solid squares with right sides together. Sew ¼" on both sides of the diagonal line. Cut on the drawn line. Press seam allowances toward the darker print and trim the dog-ears at corners.

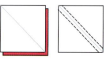

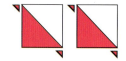

Center Unit

1. Partial seam construction: Place a yellow center square right sides together on the end of a red rectangle. Sew this seam, stopping halfway through the square, as shown, and secure with a small backstitch. Lightly press only the sewn part of the seam toward the rectangle.

2. Across the finished end of this unit, align another red rectangle, right sides together. Sew this seam. Continue clockwise around the center square.

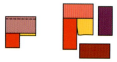

3. When you get back to the loose edge of the first rectangle, align the free edge and sew to complete the center block.

Center unit measures 4½" × 4½".

46 Chapter 2

ASSEMBLY

1. Lay out the four half-square triangles, 4 squares, and the center block. Sew into rows, pressing the seams toward the squares. Pinning together at seam intersections, sew the rows together to create the finished block. Press seams in one direction. Block measures 12½" × 12½".

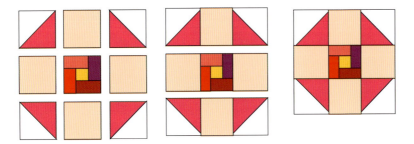

BLOCKS NEEDED FOR EXPERIENCE QUILT

12" Constant Classic blocks *make 4 blocks*

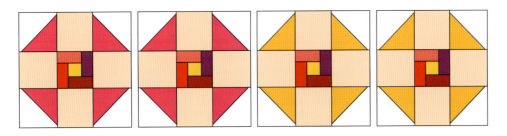

EXTRA BITS NEEDED FOR EXPERIENCE QUILT

4" Center units *make 8 units*

Half-Square Triangle units *make 4 units*

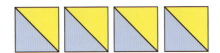

Traditions

Threads of Traditions

A LONG LINE

I've been a quilt maker for more than 40 years. One might say I was born to make quilts, but we'll get to that shortly. I started my first quilt the summer before my senior year in college. I had a host of cotton scraps from cotton frocks I'd made in the previous few years. I pulled out a Dover book on quilt blocks and started to work with my scissors, pencil, and cardboard templates. My mother walked through the guest room that served as the sewing room and asked me what I was doing. "I'm making a quilt," says I. "Why?" she asked. I wasn't sure what to say, except that I needed to. I finished up the quilt top, quilted it, and took it back with me for my last year of college.

I continued to make quilts and haunt quilt shops, as one does. One day I came across a book in a bargain bin titled *Stitched from the Soul*, which was a book of quilts made by enslaved quilt makers. I flipped through the book and came upon a photograph of Jane Arthur Bond and a number of quilts she had made. I knew that Jane was my great-great-grandmother, but I had never known she was a quilter. I asked my father about it, and he didn't know either, but he told me that his grandmother Louvinia had made quilts, and he showed me a few of them. More about Louvinia in a bit. I wrote to the author of the book and asked about Jane's quilts, since we on our side of the family knew nothing about them. I did not receive an answer, but some time later I found out that the quilts in the book were in the possession of the family of the man who had owned and impregnated Jane, and from whom we all take our last name. I later made contact with one of his descendants. We "Bonded" over the quilts, and I did eventually end up with one of Jane Bond's quilts.

Since digging in book bins at quilt shops had proved so fruitful, I continued to do so, and one day I found a copy of *Soft Covers for Hard Times* by Merikay Waldvogel. There I found Ruth Clement Bond, whom I also recognized as family. Ruth was married to J. Max Bond, who worked for the Tennessee Valley Authority in Alabama in the 1930s. While there, she designed quilts, which were stitched up by the women in the work camps. Her quilt design "Lazy Man" was voted one of the 100 best quilts of the 20th century. I saw Ruth at a family reunion in 1996, at which point she was suffering some symptoms of dementia. When I showed her the book and the quilt shown in it, she smiled broadly and said she had forgotten all about those quilts, but the memory seemed to bring her great pleasure, and we chatted about it for some time.

Not all of my family's quilt story is from book bins. Some comes from the quilts I saw on beds growing up and things my father told me. Louvinia Cleckley was my great-grandmother, and it was she who made the quilts of my childhood. My father told me that his mother, Rosabelle, always felt that Louvinia had favored her sister Bertha, and this fed a deep feeling for Rosabelle. When Louvinia died, Rosabelle took all the quilts and hid them away. When my father died, we found a dozen of Louvinia's quilts in the basement. It was as though my father was still hiding them away as directed by his mother.

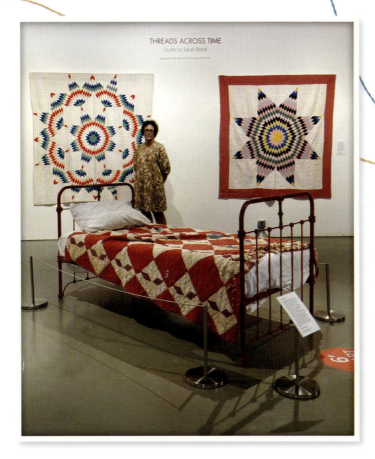

The presence of all these quilts and all these women in my head and my heart has greatly influenced my quilt making over the years. Sometimes the influence is purposeful, as when I took it upon myself to work in a series based on Louvinia's Lone Star quilts, and let my mind and my fingers run over her designs to take them to new conclusions. While communing with Louvinia and her quilts, I almost heard her sometimes. I suddenly realized that she was born in 1858, and I was born in 1958, and here we were, a century apart, working in the same medium with the same designs.

Listening to these voices and riding the commingled waves of their inspiration and my own creative direction has been a joy. I count myself lucky to know so much about my foremothers and at the same time share a passion with them. More recently, my cousin e Bond has begun designing fabric. It is an added thrill to be able to collaborate with another living descendant of this family passion. Leaning on and leaning into the legacy and vision of so many brilliant Black women is nourishing and electrifying. Now I know the answer to the question my mother asked me so many years ago. Why? Because this is what we do.

Sarah Bond

THE WEDDING QUILT

My great-grandmother Clara Collins was an artist. Her enthusiasm for textiles of all kinds was evident in her daily practices of sewing, quilting, crochet, and garment making. Her desire to pass this enthusiasm on to us, her grandchildren, came in the form of a double-wedding-ring quilt she made, to be given to the first grandchild to marry. "I will be there in spirit when you receive it," she said. Years later, I would be the first grandchild to marry, take professional quilting classes, and carry on the legacy she created of intergenerational connection, visual artistry, and storytelling.

Mary Louise Sims

SAVES LIVES

Quilts are often inspired by something personal we have experienced. They may be about someone we know or a place we have visited. But our quilts may also do the opposite—they may influence how we move forward in our life, instead of reflecting on our past. Our quilts may inspire the behavior of others who see them.

In 1982, I made a quilt named "Giving Blood Saves Lives," inspired by a postage stamp promoting blood donations. This motivated me to become a regular donor. I hope that the quilt has inspired others as it has been hanging in a hospital since 1992.

Teresa Barkley

SCRAPS!

Attending the Lancaster Quilt Show many years ago, I found myself standing outside the classroom of Kaffe Fassett. At the time, my fabric budget couldn't stretch to afford his luscious bold designs. I drooled as I peeked in the classroom and saw all the students' stashes. My head was spinning with quilt designs.

And then the impossible happened! Class was over and it was time to clean up. I watched in *horror* as these crazy people tossed their amazing Kaffe Fassett scraps into the trash! It took every ounce of willpower not to burst into the room and begin digging through the scraps.

I still remember that moment, all these years later. Fortunately, my budget now allows the purchase of his (and many others') fabric lines . . . but I still savor every scrap, no matter how small.

Deb Hunter

UNEXPECTED

I received a family heirloom from my grandmother. It was a quilt—hand pieced and hand quilted. It's a simple pattern of squares, although some of the squares are pieces of the same cloth pieced together to make a square, four by four. All the fabrics are muted pastel-colored velvet of peach, lavender, and ivory. My grandmother explained that they lived down the street from a funeral home and were given the scraps of velvet from the lining of the coffins.

Ann Barnes

ATTIC TREASURES

Twenty-six Dahlia Star blocks were created by my maternal grandmother, Marie Swartwood. She died in 1950, when my mom was just 13 years old. Amazingly, the blocks survived a number of moves—my grandfather was a preacher in Pennsylvania, and moves were typical and often. Mom claimed the blocks in the late '70s, when the attic in the Philipsburg home was being cleaned out. We reviewed them a few weeks before she died in 2013; she said she had never taken them out of the box and laid them all out together as I did that day. I can only assume that each time she opened the box and flipped through the blocks, she was overwhelmed with the task at hand, and perhaps some memories as well. Mom recalled a few of the fabrics—some from feed sacks—and the garments that she, her mother, and her sister Priscilla had worn.

I sent pictures of all the blocks to my aunt, and she also remembered. Here's the email reply I got:

"Oh Heather, what a gift you have given me! I remember the blue fabric with cherries. Mom made herself a three-quarter coat to wear over her dress when she worked at Penney's in Franklin, Pennsylvania. It had a collar and buttons down the front. She really looked great in it! We lived in Maple Dale and Dad was pastor [both] of Maple Dale and North Sandy. I had a dress made of the white with pink roses; I've seen pictures of me in it. The blue and white looks familiar—perhaps another dress. The tiny green squares look familiar, too."

Isn't it amazing the memories that a piece of fabric can evoke almost 65 years later?

Each block was made up of 25 pieces; none lay very flat, points were off, edges not even, and the whites varied, along with a few stains. A friend finally convinced me that the blocks needed to be taken apart and reconstructed—a daunting task; handwork is not my specialty! Family members helped with ripping out seams—straight seams done on machine, and curved seams for the petals, which had been done by hand—with double thread. We stopped short of disconnecting petals and star points from the center circle. I ended up with these rather limp octopus-looking things. I soaked them in vinegar to set the dye, gently washed and rinsed, and then starched and pressed each dahlia star back into shape.

After much machine embroidery, stuffing, and hand sewing, "Stars" took shape! This project felt more like an engineering project than sewing! Each block took about five hours to reconstruct.

It was done in time to celebrate my aunt's 80th birthday (2014) with the entire family. She was surprised and thrilled with the wall hanging and immediately got a friend to help her hang it horizontally over the head of her bed. There have been many phone calls since then, and she still exclaims how she loves it and how beautiful it is.

Heather Maslen

Q: Tell me when you began to quilt.

Well, I married into this community forty-five years ago and had a sewing bee that you'd come and have dinners. Then the ladies would quilt. They would make garments and I kind of watched the quilters a little bit. They were always anxious to get somebody to help them. And so they were really good to me, to help me. I'd be upset about what I had or what I'd done, but I noticed that when you quilted there, they kind of kept an eye on you. They sort of looked over your shoulder. So I tried to shorten up my stitches as soon as I could, because you need to do that to match theirs. Because if it's sold you don't want long stitches, you want short stitches. And then that's the way it's today, you have to practice. They have people practice until they are ready to pass inspection. [*Laughs.*]

[…] My mother-in-law said, "You know, Mary, quilting is a really, really bad hobby for a young mother." And I knew that, I mean it takes time. And of course you have a quilt up, and these kids are running around bumping it and getting it dirty and that kind of thing. But we had three boys, and we had them right away when we got married. And they would be so good to my quilts, and their friends would come over and they'd say, "Oh, is that a trampoline?" [*Laughs.*] And they'd say, "Oh, no, don't touch it." [*Laughs.*] I'd started work when my last boy was in kindergarten. I was a nurse, and I worked two days a week. And so I could cheat. I could work, I could quilt in the morning, and sometimes a little into the afternoon, go to my three-to-eleven shift and get my quilting done. And then we quilted every month, and so I was just in seventh heaven. And my mother-in-law and I would come together and quilt, and go home together. And I miss her now. But I learned by Aunt Bertina. She lived right across the way here, and she was my husband's great aunt. And my mother-in-law said, "If you want to learn to quilt, Mary, I'll ask Aunt Bertina over, if you want to make a quilt top," and I made a baby quilt top. I made it in blue, and we have three boys, so that was just perfect. And it was very, well, it wasn't exactly primitive, but it was very basic. We just sat there, my sister-in-law, and my mother-in-law, and Aunt Bertina and I, and quilted away until I think we were all doing very well on the first try. [*Laughs.*] Of course it takes practice.

Mary Ellen Tjossem
interviewed by Amy Henderson for the Quilt Alliance's Quilters' Save Our Stories (QSOS) project, May 25, 2003
www.qsos.quiltalliance.org/items/show/1690

OLD IS NEW AGAIN

When I was a child, my mom purchased a few yards of Christmas fabric. It was just a thin cotton, but it was a pretty print, so she made Christmas stockings for her children. Those stockings were either filled with goodies or hung for a holiday decoration. Years later, she was giving things away and she thought one of her grandsons would love to do something creative with them. He took them, but he really had no interest in them, so he turned around and gave them to me. Honestly, I really didn't have an interest in those flimsy things either.

A few months later I made a holiday-looking quilt, but it had a few squares that didn't match, so I tossed the unfinished piece to the side. Then one day I had a stroke of genius. What if I cut the three stockings in half to make six? That was easy. I got the quilt top back out of storage and discovered that I could lay those six stocking pieces atop the mismatched pieces and no one would ever know. Perfect. I put the quilt together, but it wasn't quite done. My parents had four children, so I made name tags for the stockings and attached them. A few weeks later I brought it over at Thanksgiving so my mom would be able to use it for her holiday decorating. When my mom opened the gift, she couldn't believe what had been done with those flimsy stockings. It was perfect.

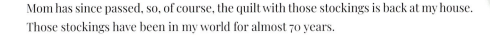

Mom has since passed, so, of course, the quilt with those stockings is back at my house. Those stockings have been in my world for almost 70 years.

June Mellinger

Q: Do you have any educational background towards quilting?

I grew up with quilts on the bed. It was just a given fact of life. I grew up Mennonite in Deer Creek, Oklahoma, where the ladies always quilted on Wednesdays, every Wednesday at the church. Even in the 1950s when quilting wasn't done in other places.

Q: So it has just been part of your life?

It has been a big part . . . I didn't have a lot of respect for quilts. We had them on every bed, and we used them up. That is what they were intended for, to keep us warm. And I still do that occasionally. I grew up around it.

[. . .] I didn't actually start quilting by myself. My mother and I made some quilts for the boys when they were tiny. I've got quilts we made in August of 1981; they are dated. And the boys still have them. But in 1987, I received a Velveeta cheese box full of diamond points that my Aunt Grace had cut out in 1967, intending to make a quilt out of them. She had pieced two of the star points for an eight-pointed star, and the rest of the diamonds were still in this cheese box. It became my heritage from Aunt Grace. I decided that over my Christmas vacation [. . .], "I am going to do this." I pieced together all the star points and then had to figure out how to set in all the squares and the triangles and put enough borders on it. It had to be king-size; every first quilter has to make a quilt that is king-size. So it was huge. I added enough borders so it fit the bed. The only two colors I could match in 1987 from 1967 were the lavender and the yellow. So when I laid it out on the bed, the first thing Ken, my husband, said was "I guess we are going to have to change the color scheme in this room?" I said, "Yeah." [*Laughter.*]

I marked the quilt, and the Deer Creek Mennonite ladies quilted it for me that following summer. I drove down on Wednesdays and quilted with them. And we sat around the quilt frame; I had my 92-year-old Great Aunt Marie on one side of me. Everybody is related who is sitting around the quilt frame. So we are quilting away, and another ninety-year-old lady across the way, Marie Wickie, said, "You know, Elsie, I think I remember quilting one like this for your Aunt Grace." That was how I found out that there was a sister quilt. I went looking for it. At another cousin's house, she and I were looking through old pictures one night. There was a photograph of the ladies at the church quilting the sister in 1967. So that was verification that there actually was a sister quilt. I went to my Aunt Grace's only son and asked about the sister quilt. Sure enough, he had it in his closet. It was tattered and worn.

Elsie Campbell
interviewed by Karen Bennick for the Quilt Alliance's Quilters' Save Our Stories (QSOS) project, October 23, 1999
www.qsos.quiltalliance.org/items/show/2478

Traditions

KEEPING TRACK

Since creating my first quilt in 2016, I have included a story with each delivered quilt explaining my fabric and pattern selection, hours/days to complete, finished size, and what I learned making the quilt. I also chose an inspirational saying to print on each label, and that saying is included in the printed quilt story. I keep these stories in a binder along with swatches of fabrics, receipts, pictures, and thank-you cards. When I want to "revisit" a friend or quilt that lives far away, I can go to this book and be reminded how I choose to express my love and how I am bringing a bit of beauty into this world.

Lori Lawrenson

MY LOVE LANGUAGE

It was Christmas. I had spent the last six weeks designing a custom quilt top representing a phospholipid bilayer—the focus of my boyfriend's PhD. Okay, so the quilt wasn't finished, but the bold graphic design was modern and striking. The points on half-square triangles lined up perfectly, and I had even incorporated his favorite color, a marine blue. He was going to love it. In my mind, this was going to be the most romantic Christmas ever!

"Oh. It's, um, big," he said flatly. And with that, I knew the relationship was basically over. I was mortified. What's more awkward? Saying I love you before the other person loves you, or making a quilt prematurely in a relationship? Oh, quilts are way more awkward! For the rest of the weekend, it sat in a messy fold on the couch. An uncomfortable reminder that I was way more invested in the relationship than he was.

In my next serious relationship, I decided to play it cool with a mini quilt. Just enough effort to say, "Hey, I think I kind of like you." But small enough to spare myself an embarrassing display of unrequited love. This time, it was a 12-inch star quilt for an astronomer I was dating. It was a simple star block against a galaxy that I free-motion quilted. He was only slightly more enthusiastic. The quilt ended up in his cat's bed. That relationship didn't last either.

After a few months of dating my next boyfriend, I hedged my bets with a tiny 3-inch mini quilt for Valentine's Day. He said he loved it and displayed it on his mantel. Was he too good to be true? That summer we moved in together. As a microbiologist, he was thrilled to find termites in our backyard. (How do I keep dating scientists?) I made him a mini quilt with termites appliquéd on it. He took it to work and put it on his desk. Later that year, I decided he was quilt worthy and invested in a full-sized quilt. It replicated a geometric pattern I saw on the cover of one of his calculus textbooks. It has fun magenta and orange diamonds. And we still use it today.

Bernadette Forward

CHAPTER 3

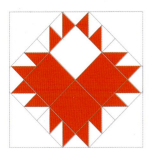

Comfort and Healing

As a child, nothing soothed my soul like a visit to my grandparents' home in southern Minnesota. There, in their cozy abode, my grandmother Elda reigned as the family's quilting queen. With hands riddled with arthritis, she skillfully crafted stunning double-knit polyester quilts that exuded love and warmth.

My grandfather, a tall drink of water, was a seasoned pro at snuggling under these quilts. I can still remember the shock of walking into the living room and seeing what appeared to be a mysterious, quilt-covered lump on the couch. Only upon closer inspection did I realize that it was my grandfather, the only person I knew who slept with the covers over his head.

Years later, when I moved to the bustling city of New York, I too found myself seeking solace under covers. To block out the noise of the city, I began sleeping with a pillow over my head. Eventually, the covers themselves became a necessary cocoon of comfort.

My family loves to poke fun at my sleeping habits, noting that I lie flat on my back with hands resting on my chest, like a headless corpse, with a pillow or quilt covering my face. But I simply smile and let them jest, knowing that these habits trace back to the memories of my beloved grandparents.

Watching my grandmother quilt brought me immense joy as I crawled beneath the quilt frame that dominated the living room. In that house, I knew only unconditional love and acceptance, a world away from the farm where I grew up, 200 miles away. When I was at home, Elda's quilts, with their double layers of polyester batting, kept me cozy and content until our next trip to my grandparents' Mississippi River town.

To this day, I have cherished figurines that conjure those feelings of being in their home, along with a massive bin of double-knit polyester. There's something truly special about these fabrics that continue to bring me comfort and security.

As quilters, we know how therapeutic the process of making a quilt can be. Colors and prints can stir strong emotions, both good and bad; the whole process allows space for healing and growth as we create. Many of us have also experienced the ways a finished quilt can provide a sense of safety and wellness. I recall sleeping on our couch with my family's "sick quilt," a quilt saved for days we missed school from seasonal maladies, snuggled under the weight of the quilt while watching daytime television until we drifted off to sleep as our bodies healed. Quilts are the best medicine—whether we are making them, giving them for others' comfort and healing, or wrapped in them ourselves!

Isn't it fascinating how even the mere sight of a stack of quilts can bring such visual pleasure, instantly calming the mind and body?

Do you have a favorite quilt that brings you comfort? Have quilts helped you heal? Perhaps you have given someone else a "quilted hug" when they needed it most.

COMFORT AND HEALING:
Bear Paw Heart Block

FOR THE 18" BLOCK:

Bear Paw Heart *red print*

 3 squares 5½" × 5½"

  4 squares 4¾" × 4¾", cut in half diagonally in both directions (16 small triangles)

Background *white print*

 1 square 5½" × 5½"

  5 squares 4¾" × 4¾", cut in half diagonally in both directions (20 small triangles)

  2 squares 8⅛" × 8⅛", cut in half diagonally (4 setting triangles)

ASSEMBLY

1. With right sides facing, sew a white-print small triangle to a red-print small triangle along the diagonal edge. Press toward the red print to create a half-square triangle and trim the dog-ears at the corners. Make 16 half-square triangles (HSTs).

2. Lay out four HSTs, a red-print square, and a white small triangle as shown, paying attention to the direction of the HSTs. Sew the HSTs together in pairs, pressing toward the red triangle.

3. Sew one pair of HSTs to a red-print square. Press toward the square. Sew a white small triangle to the other HST pair. Press toward the triangle.

4. Sew the HST/triangle unit to the HST/square unit. Press toward the square.

5. Repeat steps 2–4 to make three bear paw units with red squares and one with a white square.

   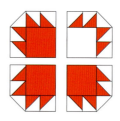

60   Chapter 3

6. Sew the bear paw units together in pairs, pressing the seam in opposite directions. Sew the pairs together to create the bear paw center.

7. Rotate the bear paw center 45 degrees and lay out the four setting triangles as shown to set the block on point. Fold the corner-setting triangles in half and finger-press to mark the center of the long diagonal edge. With right sides facing, align the diagonal edges of the triangle and the bear paw, matching the centers of both pieces. Pin in place, sew, and press toward the triangle (or open to avoid show-through).

8. Continue with the other three diagonal sides of the bear paw center unit. Block measures 18½" × 18½".

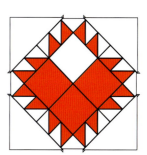

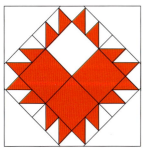

BLOCKS NEEDED FOR EXPERIENCE QUILT

18" Bear Paw Heart blocks *make 4 blocks*

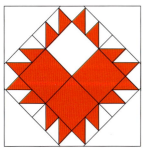 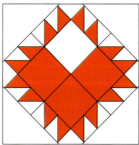 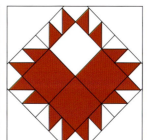 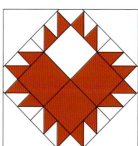

Comfort and Healing

Threads of Comfort and Healing

A VISUALIZED QUILTING PARTY

When you have radiation to the head or neck, a custom-made mask using a firm plastic mesh is molded to fit your face and upper torso. During the treatment, the mask is bolted to the table at multiple sites to ensure you remain in position. It may be saving your life, but it is also tight and claustrophobic. You can see only a little bit, straight up in front of you.

Because of a childhood trauma, the anticipation of this mask after a lymphoma diagnosis made me particularly frantic. I cried every time I thought about it. When offered the chance to learn a self-hypnosis technique, I was skeptical but willing.

The social worker was the first person in the hospital who wanted to know who I was when I wasn't a patient. She'd looked up my website and wanted to talk quilts. She was knowledgeable and spoke very quickly, and, in my exhaustion, every comment seemed simultaneously mundane and brilliant, gone from my memory as soon as she passed on to the next suggestion.

But one technique involving a crucial physical trigger grabbed me: touch your thumb to your forefinger and circle that finger against your thumb, making curlicues—which has always been both my go-to doodle and my hair's natural tendency. Each time you mentally move from thinking about one item to another, you switch to coiling the next finger against your thumb.

I decided that every day, lying bolted to the table, in my mind I would visit our vacation house on the bay. On the first day of radiation, frantically curling my fingers and listening to a CD, I visualized floating ghostlike from room to room, conscious of the giant machines zapping and banging above me. By day 3, my feet touched the floor. I got ready to take a bath in the beautiful new tub. First curlicue, get my bathrobe. Middle finger: look for matches so I could light candles (which I have never done once for a bath in real life). Ring finger: try to remember how to start the jets. Another day my daughter and I baked cookies, me coiling furiously to catch up when she looked for butter or checked to see if we owned cookie sheets.

Then came imagining a sweet week of small get-togethers, curating quilt friends from around the world. I even planned the menu, serving local Catapano honey goat cheese on Wheat Thins with Paumanok Assemblage in gold-tinged wine glasses.

First up in my mind, the two Sues I'm so fond of: Benner (Texas) and Nickels (Michigan). Even though their quilt aesthetics are very different, I knew they'd like each other a lot. Since I'm terrible at opening a bottle of wine, I sheepishly asked a Sue to do the honors.

I met my next envisioned guest in the mid-1990s, teaching at the Minnesota Quilt Festival, when I wandered into a booth filled with gorgeous overdyed goodies and met Wendy Richardson. Finally, I got to show her the view of the bay, albeit in my head. On the screened-in porch, I lounged around with Katie Pasquini Masopust (California) and our mutual friend from Spain, Rosario Casanovas, listening to the loud, rapid chirps of the baby osprey, even though it was February.

I first met quilt journalist Naomi Ichikawa (Tokyo) when she visited my city apartment in 1991 and I served her first-ever bagel and lox, naively assuming that lox was like sushi. Since that first interview, when Naomi left the Bronx with a bagel recipe, we've had amazing food adventures around the world. This time I imagined welcoming Naomi to the house and serving a commemorative bagel smeared with cream cheese.

Of course, the Quilters had to come. That's what my family calls the important threesome who take up residence a couple of weeks each year, shlepping sewing machines and paraphernalia, rearranging the furniture, and cooking fabulous meals. Katherine Knauer (New York City), Robin Schwalb (Brooklyn), and my cousin Amy Orr (Pennsylvania). But when I tried to step out the front door to walk with them to the beach, the facade fell apart, my eyes opened, and I was back in the noisy, clanging radiation room.

Needing an idea for the next session, I looked at photos from the renovation, noting my mother's seashell collection, her yard sale finds, her midcentury modern collection of chairs. My mother! I would invite my mother, who had died eighteen months before, to see the renovation of the house she loved. She liked that we knocked down the walls and got rid of the mold. "But," she asked in my head, "why did you need a new refrigerator? Wasn't the old one good enough?"

Why did I take the mask—this emotionally fraught object—home when treatment was over? Because one of the many gifts of my quilting life is the creative community of makers who surround and encourage me. I've always admired their impulse to generate art from found objects even if I wasn't quite there yet. When I retrieved the mask from the top of a closet five years later, my close friend Katherine Knauer was at my side. Seeing the silhouette again made me a bit wobbly, so Katherine covered the recognizable mesh with material from one of my fabric collections. Then I could take over.

This deeply personal work is a radical departure for me, an attempt to transform something associated with a deeply frightening and unsettling experience into an object of art and beauty using the familiar gentleness of hand beading and kaleidoscopic fabrics designed by me.

Now I refer to my embellished mask as She. When She's not traveling to exhibitions, She lives in our living room, where I can see her every day.

Paula Nadelstern

SNUGGLE QUILT?

In 1986, my quilt "Bright Hopes, Bright Promise" was selected to represent Wisconsin in the Great American Quilt Festival, in honor of the Statue of Liberty Centennial. The entire collection of 51 quilts, including mine, traveled internationally for three years under the auspices of the Museum of American Folk Art of New York.

One of my favorite stories involving this quilt happened when I completed it and removed it from the frame. My five-year-old son asked if the "new snuggle blanket" was finished. As he curled up on the couch, I covered him with the Liberty quilt, and he promptly cuddled in and fell asleep. It was probably the only quilt in this particular collection that had been slept under, but after all, that's what quilts are for!

Carol Butzke

A HEALING HUG

Early in 2023, I attended a quilt retreat with 24 women in San Rafael, California, a perfect way to start the new year.

The stormy weather in Northern California had caused many problems, including flooding, fallen trees, and power outages, which led to a young woman being displaced and staying at the hotel. She noticed one of us wearing a quilt-themed sweatshirt in the restaurant and asked about it, which led to her learning about our retreat and the quilters gathered there. We invited her to come and visit. The young woman walked into the ballroom and immediately burst into tears, overwhelmed with emotion. "You're quilters! Just like my mom," she exclaimed. The women got up from their seats and hugged her as she cried. She explained that she had recently lost her mother, who was an avid quilter and a founding member of the Marin Quilt Guild. She had donated more than 80 of her mother's quilts and missed her terribly. She asked if anyone knew her mother, and went from table to table, admiring our work and sharing stories about her mother, crying and hugging all the while. Her mother had loved retreats with her quilt friends, and her entire life was all about quilting.

Another quilter returned to the room and was quickly updated on what was happening. She walked over to the young woman and said, "I knew your mother." She had lived in Marin, been on retreats with her, been to her house, and even met her siblings years ago. She had pictures on her phone! It was surreal. We all cried, amazed at how quilting can bring people together.

What the young woman needed couldn't be bought or easily found, but her mother had led her to us, a group of women quilters at a retreat where she could receive the hug she so desperately needed, filled with love from quilters just like her mom. It was a hug that told her she was home and that everything was going to be okay. Quilters are special people who touch lives all the time.

Laurie Parry

Chapter 3

AN UNEXPECTED GIFT

In 2014, I received the best gift of all—a handmade quilt that was created with love when I was diagnosed with breast cancer. Even today, the colorful and vibrant quilt adorns our family room and will be treasured for as long as I live. What makes this quilt so special is that it was pieced together with blocks contributed by people from all around the world, creating a kaleidoscope of color. To me, quilts are like masterpieces of art, with their intricate patterns, varied colors, and stitching that holds everything together. Although I'm not a quilter myself, I truly appreciate the beauty and craftsmanship that goes into every quilt.

Claire Deslongschampes

SEWED TOGETHER

Sorry for my bad English. It is not my mother language.

My third son is autistic. When he was very young, our family life was very difficult. Often he was angry; he had crises. I remember when he was four and a half years old, he lived a troubled time, and when he used to have a difficult moment, we used to sit in front of my sewing machine, and we used to sew together squares. He held the fabric, and I pushed the sewing machine.

So we made a quilt for him. The center of the quilt was Winnie the Pooh; my son loved him a lot. When the quilt was made, he slept under it. Sewing squares made my son more quiet and the family life better.

Now, I am writing this story and my thirty-year-old autistic son is near me and is supervising my text. (And said just now: "Exactly!" . . . and laughs at my parentheses.)

Gladys Manzanares

STITCHES

Being told you have a brain tumor is gut wrenching enough, but running late for the first appointment to meet the doctor who is going to remove it really made my blood pressure skyrocket.

During the appointment, Dr. Roland asked many questions, not only medical but about my life as well. When I mentioned I was a quilter, he looked up at me and smiled. He told me he was raised in Lancaster, Pennsylvania.

After surgery I returned to Dr. Roland to have the stitches removed. I asked, "Out of curiosity, how many stitches were there?"

Comfort and Healing

"One," he replied.

"One?"

"Yes, I used a running stitch," he said with a smile.

Deb Hunter

CAMP FIRE SURVIVOR

Born in the 1950s, I was fortunate to have grown up during simpler times. My family was middle class, with a hardworking father and a stay-at-home mother who sewed all day long. As a child, I was surrounded by my sisters' love for Elvis and the sound of my mother's sewing machine. I didn't appreciate it then, but I do now—the pretty homemade dresses, complete with big bows at the waist and matching bows in the hair. I believe the ritual of sewing is ingrained in my DNA.

When our home was lost in the 2018 Camp Fire in Paradise, California, I was devastated. The fear, depression, and anxiety were overwhelming. It took me almost a year to gather the tools and strength to sit down and stitch. In lieu of therapy and medication prescribed by my doctor, I turned to creating quilts in my quiet spare room. The hum of the sewing machine and the memories of watching my mother create quilts and all things fabric over the decades brought me joy I thought I had lost. It has been four years since that fateful day. I now have a new home, new town, new state, and new friends. I have found solace in my old self sitting and creating, and I smile at the close to 108 quilts I have made as therapy in this new place. Fabric, thread, and a sewing machine have been the best therapy for me.

Cheryl Wilkinson

Q: *Tell me about the quilt. [. . .] And what was the origin?*

I made the quilt when I moved to Colorado, while my daughter was going through chemotherapy and radiation therapy for breast cancer. It not only gave me peace when I needed it the most, when I stopped crying long enough. But it opened up a whole other side of it because every time I show the quilt now, people tell me their cancer story and it is just—it's like a healing process for me. It was a really important quilt in my life and maybe not the best one I've ever made, but certainly the most meaningful one I've made.

[. . .] I call it "Ribbons of Hope."

Q: *What was the pattern? Describe the pattern and the colors.*

Actually I made it up. Because I knew that everybody was giving me the pink ribbons when my daughter was going through this, and I must have about six or seven of different pink ribbons. So, I knew I wanted to make a quilt in which the ribbon was an important thing because I think in our society now everything has a ribbon. You know when the soldiers go overseas, you have a yellow ribbon. So I started doodling and I came up with that pattern, just by doodling and having it look like ribbons are flowing across it, the surface.

[. . .] I pieced the basic one and then I took organza ribbons and went across in the opposite direction, so to speak. So ribbons on ribbons, I guess.

[. . .] As we were sitting at the many places where she would have chemotherapy, I started talking to people. Somebody would have a green ribbon, somebody would have a pink ribbon, and before I made the quilt I was sort of asking them what that meant, and really learned a lot, because they are very fanatic about the kind of cancer they go to, obviously, and then they would say, "Well this ribbon means da-da-da-da." So it could be prostate cancer, it could be lung cancer; they all have a different color. And I didn't know that.

[. . .] I think I'm going to donate it to the place where my daughter had chemotherapy. I'm just sort of enjoying it for a while. But I think it will be a fun place to hang on the wall where they sit for so many hours and have something to look at. That's my hope for it.

Louisa L. Smith
interviewed by Joanne Gasperik for the Quilt Alliance's Quilters' Save Our Stories (QSOS) project, August 3, 2003
www.qsos.quiltalliance.org/items/show/2098

HOW TO QUILT A LIFE

I rode to the hospital that night in the front seat of a police car. Usually, my husband accompanied me for emergency room visits, and we rehearsed my stories en route. This time, I traveled in silence.

The doctor kept lights low within the glass-fronted exam cubicle, describing petechial hemorrhaging in my eyes and fresh bruising around my neck to the nurse taking notes. The investigating officer stood in the corner. I withered into my own embrace.

"I'm cold," I whispered. My clothes were drenched with sweat; it hurt to speak. The nurse retrieved clean scrubs and a warmed blanket; the doctor and officer stepped out so I could change. But as the nurse peeled off my blouse, she called for the doctor, and instead of helping me into the scrubs, they measured and photographed a patchwork of bruises on my torso, arms, and legs. In hushed voices, they analyzed colors ranging from purplish black to dark blue, from green fading to yellow, estimating the age of each contusion.

Before I was discharged from the hospital the next day, my husband was arraigned on felony domestic assault charges and released from the county jail. A no-contact order meant I could return to the parsonage and he could not. The house was eerily quiet. I lost myself in the repetitive motion of hand quilting, finding solace in the forgiving nature of fabric and thread.

I'd learned to piece quilts almost 30 years earlier, using cutting scraps from garment making: floral fragments from the dress I made to wear to my husband's 1987 ordination, bright cottons from clothing made for my children, and leftover fabrics chosen by others who hired me to sew.

But trauma is a leech that sucks creative energy, and my quilts became less imaginative over time with each spirit-crushing verbal assault, bruise, and broken bone. When news stories identified the United Methodist pastor arrested for strangling an unnamed victim at the parsonage on Country Club Road, where nothing like this had ever happened before, I felt exposed. Invisible. Alone.

Comfort and Healing

Until the quilters arrived. Jean came with flowers, lattes, and blueberry muffins. Her husband, Bob, offered fabric from his stash. "I don't know how else to support you," he said through tears I cherish because I could not cry.

Bob and Jean invited me to sew with them and a group of their quilting friends at an upcoming weekend retreat. I didn't know any of the others attending, but they welcomed me into their close-knit community. While I waited my turn at the cutting table or pressing station, these new friends examined my piecework. They buoyed my confidence and reinvigorated my imagination. They included me in banter and storytelling. Best of all, we laughed. There was so much joy stitching with these quilters, who offered me a safe place to land.

For three days I gulped creative energy like someone rediscovering oxygen. I pieced these moments into Lady of the Lake blocks and sketched birds flitting through twisting vines and leaves to appliqué along the quilt's future borders. By Sunday afternoon, when it was time to pack up our works in progress and return to the lives we'd left behind, my quilt top—originally planned as a wall hanging—had quadrupled in size because my new friends contributed scraps from their own work to enhance mine. This experience became the thread I needed to begin the daunting task of stitching my broken world into a new story. I'd lived for three decades as a bird who forgot she had wings. My quilting friends reminded me what it means to soar.

Millie K. Kehrli

A SPECIAL LABEL FOR A SPECIAL GIFT

This is the note that goes with the quilts the women receive at Limen House:

When I was a child, my great-grandmother made me a quilt. I loved all of the colors and patterns. I remember hiding under my quilt, looking up, expecting darkness, but instead, seeing all the colors come through—a kaleidoscope of fabric. Just a blanket, but it filled me with wonder, and it was always there for me. No matter what happened, or where it happened, that quilt was there. It didn't suddenly change or leave; it was always there.

The quilt you have in front of you isn't great; it is probably one of the first I have ever made. Some look "prettier" than others, some are made better than others, but each one is special in its own way. I know one in particular has holes (I did stitch the holes btw)! But guess what, I didn't give up on that quilt. Some I made do with what I had, even if it didn't work out for the best. And for that, I love each one of them. They all taught me something or showed me something I didn't know before.

And most of all, each one was made with the intent of giving you something my quilt gave me as a child, comfort and security. Thank you for accepting my quilts as they are—works in progress.

Trissa Hill

CHAPTER 4

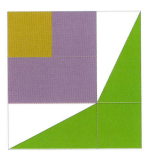

Connection

Quilting has long been associated with creating and fostering connections within communities. Historically, women would gather to work on quilts together, sharing stories, ideas, and techniques. Quilting bees were not just a chance to create beautiful and functional objects, but also a way for people to connect and support one another.

Today, quilting continues to provide a sense of community and belonging for everyone. Quilt guilds and groups exist all over the world, where quilters come together, in person or online, to share their passion, knowledge, and experiences.

I met my dearest friend, Helen, when we sat next to each other at the Empire Quilt Guild. The experience of showing your work to others can be nerve wracking, especially when you are new to a group like a quilting guild. I remember feeling terrified to go up for show-and-tell with my quilt, but thankfully Helen gently encouraged me to take the plunge, even though we had just met.

Despite my fears, I shared my quilt with the group. Something magical happened as I stood there sharing my work! I felt a sense of connection and community that I had never experienced before. People came up to me afterward, admiring my quilt and asking about my process. I suddenly realized that I wasn't a lone newcomer anymore—I had found my tribe.

This is one of the amazing things about quilting guilds and communities. By coming together and sharing our work, we create connections and build relationships that can last a lifetime. No matter how nervous or unsure you may feel about sharing your work, remember that there is a group of people out there who will appreciate it and support you. So take that first step, share your work, and like-minded folks will find you!

Having quilting as a passion gives us many opportunities to find connection. We have a way to find each other easily in almost every big city around the world. Having the internet, we can find people who understand us, from all walks of life.

I am personally drawn to people who make me giggle. My closest friends in my sewing circle know how to bring me to tears of laughter. Our quilt retreats are never short on fun and are filled with silly shenanigans. I find this kind of connection priceless. I'm so grateful that this community exists.

What do you value about your quilting connections? What do you look for when you want to make a new connection or join a new quilting group? What unexpected connections has quilting given you that have brought joy to your life?

Connection

CONNECTION: Floris Block

TIP: When you need to cut pieces that are directional (like right-leaning and left-leaning triangles), cutting one template from a folded piece of fabric will yield you one of each direction.

FOR THE 6" BLOCK:

Flower Center *solid gold*

1 square 2½" × 2½"

Flower *bright print*

1 square 2½" × 2½"

1 rectangle 2½" × 4½"

Leaves *green print*

1 triangle, left triangle template

1 triangle, right triangle template

1 square 2½" × 2½"

Background *white background print*

1 triangle, left triangle template

1 triangle, right triangle template

ASSEMBLY

1. Sew the flower center square to the flower square; press the seam allowance toward the flower square. Sew the flower rectangle to the bottom of this unit, as shown. Press seam allowance toward the rectangle.

2. With right sides together, align the diagonal edges of the leaf left triangle and the background left triangle, matching the dog-ear ends as shown. Sew along the diagonal edge. Press seam allowances toward the leaf.

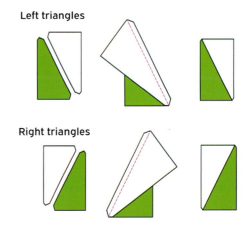

3. Repeat step 2 with the leaf right triangle and background right triangle.

4. Follow diagram to arrange the flower, leaf units, and leaf square. Sew the left leaf triangle unit to the bottom of the flower and press seam allowance toward the flower.

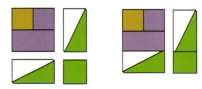

5. Sew the right leaf triangle unit to a leaf square, pressing seam allowance toward the square.

6. Align this unit right sides together with the flower / left leaf unit, pinning the leaf/square points together.

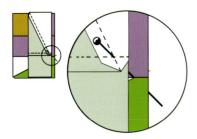

TIP: To pin the leaf points together, stick a pin straight down through the point (seam intersections) of one piece, then through the same point of the other. While that pin is standing straight through the points, place a pin in the usual way on both sides of the standing pin so the fabric doesn't shift.

Sew this seam and press seam allowance toward the leaf/square unit to complete the flower block. Block measures 6½" × 6½".

BLOCKS NEEDED FOR EXPERIENCE QUILT

6" Floris blocks *make 6 blocks*

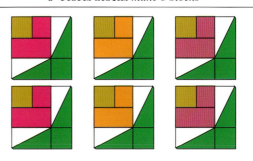

12" Floris blocks *make 2 blocks*

Make and arrange four 6" Floris blocks as shown, paying attention to the direction of each block.

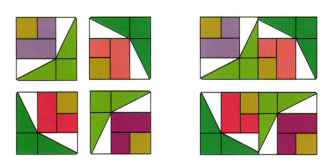

Sew the blocks together in pairs, pinning to match the points. Press seam allowances open. Sew the pairs together and press seam allowance open. Block measures 12½" × 12½".

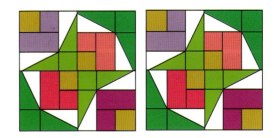

Connection

75

Threads of Connection

QUILTED CONNECTIONS

How could someone enjoy cutting fabric into a million pieces and sewing it all back together? I didn't understand at first. After seeing the joy that quilting brought my wife, Kelsey, and the connection it formed between her and her mom, I didn't have to understand. It was apparent that quilting was a positive outlet, and I wanted to encourage my best friend. After all, we were getting married in a few short months.

I knew Kelsey was serious about quilting when she asked me if we could have a quilt as our wedding backdrop. She and her mom had a favorite quilter whose double-wedding-ring pattern was "perfect." Kelsey and her mom would bond in the year leading up to the wedding over cutting shapes, sewing curved lines, and renting longarm time together to bring the project to life.

I knew I wanted to surprise Kelsey with a new sewing machine for her wedding gift, but I had no clue where to start. Her mom would know, but I wanted to keep it a secret, so I didn't want to ask her. That exhausted the list of quilters in my life.

What about that quilter lady they like? What if I messaged her on Instagram? How cool would it be to get a recommendation from Kelsey's favorite quilter? She has tens of thousands of followers, so who knows if she'll answer . . . but it's worth a shot.

What do you know—before long I had a reply from *the* Victoria Findlay Wolfe. She gave me a machine recommendation and contact information for a place to get a good deal. She was kind, engaging, and sincere!

Our wedding day came, and Kelsey loved her gift! The machine was a hit, but even more so was the story behind it. I couldn't thank Victoria enough for contributing to our special day. Afterward, we sent a card and wedding favor to Victoria, thinking it might be our final interaction.

You can imagine how bewildered I was to see Victoria walk into our craft studio just a couple of years later. We spent the day talking, and it all came full circle as I got to take a picture of Kelsey and Victoria with our wedding quilt. We stayed in touch through the years, and our internet quilter artist friend became our real friend and supporter.

What I understand now is that quilting isn't just about cutting fabric into a million tiny pieces and sewing them back together. It's more than artistic expression using a fabric medium. The feelings of love, warmth, and support that come with being wrapped up in a quilt are the same feelings that come from the people in the quilting community.

Ryan Danley

RECOGNITION AND LEGACY

I have been a quilter for 30-plus years, and I am a third-generation quilter. However, it skipped the second! But my mom always admired my work even if she had never tried it herself.

I am self-taught, but I believe the quilt gene came from my nana, Flora Chilcote. I am the third-youngest grandchild in my family, so my nana was much older when I came along, but she encouraged me to sew. She tried to teach me to make clothing, as she was an amazing seamstress. I think her skill was born of necessity, as she helped to support the family through the Great Depression with her work. When the railroad laid off workers, my pop-pop was out of a job. Every little bit helped. That seamstress gene did not land in my DNA but has skipped to one of my nieces, who is a talented seamstress.

Quilts were meant to be used for warmth, so any quilts that we had were washed and loved, and only one still remains. I found it in the trunk of my father's car in 1987 and asked the story behind it. It was a wedding gift from my great-grandparents to my parents in 1946. It is not pretty to the average person, as it is made of upholstery fabric, suiting, flannel, and so on. But there was something more important in it that I did not discover until 2013.

My mom passed away in 2012, and I was preparing to make a portrait quilt of her high school graduation portrait. I was using the photo when I saw something exciting. I was sure that her suit fabric was familiar, but how?

I ran to the quilt on the wall. There it was! A piece of my mom's suit. I began to cry and could not stop fingering the fabric. My nana made so many of my mom's clothes and all of her underclothes when she went to nursing school in 1941. I was part of all of that legacy. I am honored and privileged.

Trisha Moller

MY ONLINE HOOKUP

Back in the day, when internet and online meet-ups were still new, I went online to meet fellow quilters. After not having success finding a group that I fit in with, I scoured the internet for a more eclectic group. I happened upon a group called NYC Metro Modern quilters. They had a meeting coming up that was held in a member's home. The kicker was that this place was in an area of NYC that I didn't know to be residential.

With safety in mind, considering I was a former prosecutor, I shared my destination with family and friends. Most of them called me crazy for meeting someone randomly online. I, on the other hand, felt the pull of brightly colored fabrics and thread. I assured them that quilters, although armed with "sew" many possible weapons, were not likely to be serial killers or mass murderers. I continue to be thankful for my instinctive pull, because through this one chance hookup, I became part of and developed with an incredible group of artisans, fabric lovers, quilters, and lovers of all things fiber. I remain forever stitched with the owner of this chance online hookup and continue to grow and cherish our friendship.

Earamichia Brown

THE LANGUAGE OF QUILTS

I thought everyone went through a quilting phase. It was inevitable that I would; all the women in my life quilted. My mother made me a split-rail fence when I graduated from college. When I studied in Germany, my aunt made me a red, white, and blue star quilt to remind me of home. More than a decade later, my mother pieced together a lap quilt from my retired camouflage uniforms.

It was my former mother-in-law who coached me through my first quilt. It was just simple squares and borders with a Christmas tree crudely appliquéd into each square. At that time, I was an active-duty Marine married to another Marine. My husband was usually deployed, and I was frequently alone when not at work. Looking back, I was lonely and in desperate need of some creative outlet. I was also homesick.

My quilting phase burned hot and bright. I made several baby quilts for friends, but my magnum opus was a schoolhouse quilt. It started as a full-size quilt but ended up nearly a queen. Ultimately, I completed only the top. I mailed it home so my mother could find someone to quilt it for me. Finally, I needed only to bind it, and yet, I carried that quilt from state to state for the next 20 years before I finally paid someone to bind it. I never made another. Even though I don't quilt anymore, I have never forgotten that language.

In January 2023, I happened across a sale listing for hex signs (Pennsylvania Dutch barn paintings). The description implied that the seller possessed "more than 50," all made by a recently deceased artist. In fact, there were 65 remaining hex signs from an estimated total of 120. These were painted by a man who spent more than two decades making folk art in his free time. So compelled was I to give this man his due and show his unique body of work in its entirety that I bought all 65 remaining signs.

My husband and I are still unraveling the mystery of the artist and his unusual body of work. Many of his hex signs are traditional in their iconography, with tulips and raindrops summoning fertility and good fortune. But his fluency in the language of quilting is undeniable. Among his works are hex signs incorporating flying geese, lone stars, trips around the world, and blanket stitches. There are also five barn quilts where he allowed himself to meld his own craft with quilting almost entirely. These are his most uninhibited and joyful works.

Although the artist was using a different medium, this man spoke that same language I learned to speak in my 20s. It was a language that afforded both of us some essential freedom of expression that we felt we did not otherwise have. And despite not having used that language personally in more than 20 years, I found I could still comprehend what his pieces were communicating.

Nicole Dubé

STRAY BLOCKS AND SISTERHOOD

In the summer of 1975, my family was in the process of moving. We had a short stay at a motel, where I first saw the "super cool" embroidered denim cutoff shorts that the Norris girls wore. They had hand-stitched flowers and bubble letters that, to this day, are seared into my creative memory. What we all didn't know as I spied them on the steps of the Holiday Inn in Morgantown, West Virginia, was that we would soon be neighbors and lifelong mates. They were four sisters, and I was the only girl in my family (although my two brothers dated a sister of their respective age), and we got along well. Even our parents were friends and shared their own friendship with their own memories, like an Oktoberfest gone sideways that the five of us can't imagine our mothers participating in!

Both of our families moved around, me an Army brat, and them hailing from Georgia with a dad who worked for a federal agency. When Atlanta was announced for QuiltCon 2023, a comfort passed through me. I remembered I had received old appliquéd quilt blocks that the girls had found while clearing out their family farm in 2018. Immediately, I found myself digging into my stash and designing a quilt I wished to enter into the show. I have never had the urge to design and submit before. But this was an inner compass directing me to use these blocks as a symbol of our 47-year friendship and our accomplishments. The embroidery thread on the blocks echoed the embroidery thread on the cutoff shorts. I had to re-create that feeling.

The blocks became a talisman, an excuse, and a reason for numerous emails, text exchanges, and phone calls. While creating my design, we shared stories, which quickly brought to light the very different ages we each were in 1975. The oldest of us exclaimed that she was positive the rest of us were referring to an alternate universe: somehow, hanging out by the old springhouse at the bottom of the sledding hill smelled very different for her group of friends than ours. But for us four younger girls, she fiercely carried the torch of womanhood forward. Almost 50 years later, we see little difference in the span of our years.

I deliberately decided to use these blocks in the quilt design to reignite our friendships. I found that these flowered blocks reminded me of the universal symbol of women. I combined the older blocks, my newer blocks, and an earlier project of mine celebrating Ruth Bader Ginsberg's collars, all of which seemed to me to be symbols of strength and unity. My quilt conveys a hope that, as women, we can stand together, even when opinions differ, because we share a common history and future. This is the story of the completion of "Herstory," the quilt that we celebrated together at QuiltCon in Atlanta in 2023.

Amy Wade

DUCK, DUCK . . .

Quilt retreats are all about sewing and forging memorable connections. Rumor has it that quilters accomplish a great deal, finishing their UFOs, completing their current project, and even beginning a new one. Personally, I've not found that to be true. It could be that I'm more intent on having fun than sewing like a madwoman.

I generally hang with people who have a wicked sense of humor and don't get angry at small stuff. Small, like finding a little rubber duck (or five) nesting on their sewing machine. Ah, the rubber ducks; therein lies a tale.

For years a group of us passed around rubber ducks like they were treasured trophies. Tiny ducks, medium ducks, ducks wearing rabbit ears, ducks wearing sewing aprons; any duck would do as long as it was portable. If one of us got up and left our sewing station, you could bet you would find a rubber duck on your sewing machine or hidden among your fabric or in your sewing case when you returned. You just didn't want to get caught "ducking" someone, so being sneaky was imperative. And lying about being the culprit that left a duck somewhere was expected and acceptable behavior.

One thing I could always count on when I put my overnight bag in my room was that someone had been there before me. I would find a multitude of rubber ducks stashed in my room. Once I even found ducks swimming in the toilet. Good thing their heads were above the waterline, because fishing them out was not on my to-do list.

It was easy to find the culprit when it came to having my room ducked. It had to be someone with a key. And I knew who had the keys to all the rooms, so I was always sure I knew whom to blame.

Then came the unforgettable year of the giant duck. I opened my door to my room, and there on my bed was a duck. Not a tiny rubber ducky, but a huge blown-up pool duck, large enough to serve as a life raft if one was drowning. It fit across both twin beds and left little room for anything else. I had trouble trying to get past the duck just to stick my overnight bag in the closet.

I stood there and pondered what action I should take. The one thing I was sure of was that this was not going to be allowed to stand! That duck was going to have to spend the weekend swimming on someone else's bed in another room, and I knew exactly which room it was going to live in.

I enlisted the friend who was acting as "room mother," since she had the master key to all the rooms. Off we went, running down the hall, duck in tow. We placed it across the twin beds in the duck's new nest, locked the door, went downstairs, and set up our sewing stations. Neither of us said a word about the giant duck. We waited patiently for the duck to be found. We were sure the women in whose room the duck was nesting would not be able to keep quiet about the giant duck. We were so wrong about that! They said nothing to anyone. So disappointing!

It took a year for the giant duck to resurface. The woman who was sharing her room with the duck decided it should make a grand entrance. She brought it down and placed it on the cutting table. It was almost as though she expected someone to fess up to putting it in her room. It was a closed-mouth bunch though, a bunch of women that laughed easily and took advantage of a funny situation and made the most of it.

I still wonder who brought that duck. Hmmm, I'll probably never find out, but that's okay, I've always loved a good mystery!

Edie McGinnis

RETREAT FUN

It's been a long-standing mystery, so should I tell the story about that time my sister and I bought a giant yellow inflatable duck pool float and set it in an unsuspecting quilt retreater's room and never fessed up to it . . . ? Nah, what fun would that be?

Katy Kitchen

SISTER RIVALRY

My sister and I were estranged for 20 years. I am the older, more successful sister, and my younger sister was very conscious of the difference in our lives and resentful of the attention I received. I have a PhD, and she worked at night in a factory.

Due to the nature of her job, she was able to sit and watch dials and do handwork. She eventually became very proficient, began appliquéing and quilting, and produced gorgeous, meticulous quilts.

When I was shown her works by my mother, I contacted my sister and asked her if she would teach me. She suggested I attend a quilt retreat with her. I went and met her friends and made myself her pupil. I copied one of her quilts and always credited her with my success. When we are together now in a quilting group and I'm asked to give my name, I say, "I am *her* sister and nowhere as good as she is."

And that is the TRUTH . . . I am not pretending. She knows it, and I know it.

We came back together as sisters because of quilting.

Lynn Brown

SMALL WORLD

When we were young parents of two girls, my husband's coworker Dan would host a picnic each year to coincide with the balloon festival in the field across from his property, which ended with fireworks. It was a gathering we looked forward to each year. One of my fondest memories was of how special his wife, Jackie, made it for the kids. She always made sure there was a special treat for each child, and her kindness has remained a dear memory throughout the years.

Fast forward to 2022: my kids are grown, and I am now a grandmother. But I still remember Jackie's kindness. My quilt guild posted a request on Facebook about a woman who is now in her 80s and not doing well and who was looking for a quilt to be made in remembrance of her sister. This woman, now widowed, had planned to have her sister, who was a quilter, come live with her, but life had different plans, and the sister passed before the move could happen.

I had a finished quilt that was looking for a home, so I contacted the requester and told her I would love to donate this quilt. My husband and I delivered it that same day, only to find out that the requester was asking for her friend and would make sure she got the quilt. If this was the end of the story it would have been enough for me, as I felt good about bringing someone else joy through my quilt.

However, it was not the end. I received a thank-you note a few days later from the new owner of the quilt; it was none other than Jackie! Later we connected by phone, and I was able to share with her how special those picnics were to my family and how happy I was to know that she received the quilt.

Geralyn Sherman

A CONNECTION TO THE PAST

In 1918, Wilhelm and Christina Bader got married. Their families had emigrated from the Odessa region of Russia (now Ukraine) and settled near Wishek, North Dakota, in the 1880s. It was an insular community of German-descended pioneers. Wilhelm and Christina moved to Eureka, South Dakota, so Wilhelm could open a meat market. They welcomed two sons within three years into their little family.

In the moments of spare time she found to herself, early in the morning or late at night by the light of a kerosene lantern, she worked on a quilt. This wasn't to be just like any other quilt. Christina made a quilt template out of paper and carefully cut triangle and diamond shapes out of scraps left over from years' worth of homemade dresses. With needle and thread, working by hand, she sewed one to the next. After a few years she had pieced a beautiful wool quilt top.

She continued the project with elaborate embroidery designs that her mother passed on to her from the Odessa region. With skill and careful choice of colors, it began to reflect her heritage and connect her to family left behind in Russia. The quilt top was nearly done when her health failed, and she came to the end of her life after three years of marriage.

Wilhelm remarried in 1923, to Dorothea Joachim. He inherited his father's farm near Wishek and returned to Wishek to take up the life of a farmer. Through the drought and the Depression, they struggled together, laboring through intense dust storms that made the days look like night. When crops did grow and there were hopes of a hearty harvest, grasshoppers descended on the fields and stripped the plants bare.

With a little bit of hope for better days ahead, Dorothea set to complete Christina's quilt in her honor and purchased fabric from the Bertsch Spitzer Family Store in Ashley, North Dakota. The fabric she used for the outer border and backing of Christina's quilt was of the new American color Nile green. The quilt is a combination of German and Ukrainian design and heritage, and the current fashion of the new country. It is a mix of the old and the new, connecting the past and the present, providing warmth to her family for generations to come.

Melanie Anderson

QUILTED CONNECTIONS

My quilting tale began when my mom organized our first Family Quilt Day in 2015. My sisters and I spent the day learning how to make a quilt from my mom. I was hooked immediately. I lived an hour away, so later, when we couldn't sew together, I would call with questions or just to talk sewing. We chatted frequently, sharing suggestions on fabric selections and thread choices.

After I got engaged later that year, I called Mom with my idea of making a double-wedding-ring quilt for my wedding backdrop. Of course, it had to be king size. The next year I would be going on countless fabric-shopping trips and sleepovers spent cutting fabric, with Mom teaching me how to sew curved seams, and taking a class together on longarm quilting. She showed me the patience it takes to lay out a plan, and helped rip out my seams on the nights I wanted to quit.

Little did I know during this time that my fiancé messaged the artist behind the pattern we were using, to get advice on purchasing my wedding gift. I was ecstatic when I opened a midarm machine before our ceremony. I joked with our photographer that I was going to leave to set it up immediately. Ryan has always been an encourager of my passions, so this gesture was no different.

Shortly after our wedding, we moved for a job, and I found myself in a new city. I leaned into quilting during this time; my Juki machine became my best friend. As I finished projects, my husband and I explored our new city to find quilt photo locations, and I gifted quilts to those closest to me to celebrate babies and weddings. I even joined my local quilt guild and attended my first quilt retreat, where I made friends and learned new techniques.

In 2019 I became the caregiver for my husband after a spinal-cord injury, and my quilting community helped me in ways I didn't know I needed. A hand-stitching project with a card arrived at the Canadian hospital where we stayed, followed by meal train dinners, care packages filled with quilting books and fabric for inspiration, and a quilt made by the guild at my first meeting back. This was about more than a hobby; it may have been thread and fabric that brought us together at first, but I gained a support system. I've learned that it's about not only sharing your latest projects and ideas, as quilters do, but also checking in on the quilter behind the machine.

Ryan and I started looking for different ways to entertain ourselves for the upcoming winter and decided on ice dyeing to create hand-dyed fabric for use in my quilts. This idea has now developed into our business, Ohio Drip. Up next on our list is teaching Ryan how to use his latest birthday present, a sewing machine from me.

Kelsey Danley

CHAPTER 5

 Aging

For many of us, quilting is not just a hobby; it is a way of life—a way of expressing ourselves, creating something beautiful, and connecting with others. It can be incredibly difficult when aging or any health event begins to impact our ability to quilt as we once did. So what happens when we start to notice our aging? How do we embrace it when we find that some of our skills are not as sharp as the new pack of needles we just bought?

When we are no longer able to quilt with the same level of skill or speed, it can feel like a part of ourselves has been taken away. It can be frustrating and disheartening to see our hands and bodies not able to do what they once did with ease. Although most of my days are spent dreaming up the next fun idea to make, that's not to say that my body hasn't had something to say. Spending a long period of time sitting at the machine, or standing and cutting fabrics, the feet, lower back, and hands scream for attention! And let's not even start to talk about just how fast time goes by the older we get.

In the last few years, my eyes have changed significantly, with cataracts and glaucoma. An ache I've had in my hand for years is now painful arthritis in my left thumb. The task of whipping down my bindings by hand, the way I prefer, once took me four hours on a king-size quilt and now takes me a week by doing an hour or less a night in a sitting. Yes, I realize that I can machine-bind them, but I will continue to do them by hand until I can't do them, since it's hard to give up that part of the process that I love—savoring those final stitches to complete a beautiful quilt.

In a class one day, as I was making my rounds to connect with each student, I came upon JoAnn, who was teary and frustrated. She shared with me that she had a stroke just a few months before, and she was finding that her hands, eyes, and coordination were just not the same as before. I felt her pain. It's not something we usually talk about in class, since we are so focused on learning something new and mastering it as well. I shared with JoAnn that it's a wonderful thing that she

was here with us anyway, and by just being with other quilters, we can support each other. The changes she was going through were going to be happening to many of us at some point. Ultimately, it didn't matter if her piece was not perfect; she—not the quilt—was the precious part of the story.

It was a great reminder to me that we must be gentle and patient with ourselves. We can celebrate our past accomplishments and be proud of what we have achieved, even if we can no longer quilt with the same level of ease. Aging may affect our skills, but it does not diminish our value as quilters or as human beings.

There are ways to adapt to changes in our abilities and still enjoy quilting. We can try new techniques or styles that are more forgiving on our hands and bodies. We can also seek out resources and support from other quilters who may have experienced similar challenges.

One of the things I have loved the most while teaching is the conversation of wisdom and knowledge that gets shared. I have learned more about women's health and aging, for which I will be forever grateful. As we share the most intimate details from hot flashes to migraines to children/grandchildren issues, and everything else in between, our bonds are formed, holding each other in strength and respect. This happens no matter who is in the class. Male and female alike, we can learn and understand each other better and make connections that show we are not alone. That is the power of quilting together.

Since that discussion with JoAnn, I've incorporated the insight she gave me as a reminder in all my workshops. At the end of my classes, I remind students that it is important to remember that our value as quilters is not solely based on our skill level or speed. We are valuable simply because we love and appreciate the art of quilting. Our experiences, our stories, and our passion for quilting are just as important as the final product. And that at a certain time in our future, the skills we learn today are going to start fading away . . . and that good enough is good enough.

Aging

AGING: Polished Diamond Block

FOR THE PIECED DIAMOND BLOCK:

Small Diamonds *bright print*

 5 diamonds, small diamond template

Small Diamonds *white print*

 4 diamonds, small diamond template

Corner Triangles *yellow print*

 2 triangles, corner triangle template

 2 triangles, corner triangle template reversed

FOR THE SOLID DIAMOND BLOCK:

Large Diamond *white print*

 1 diamond, large diamond template

Corner Triangles *navy print*

 2 triangles, corner triangle template

 2 triangles, corner triangle template reversed

PIECED DIAMOND BLOCK ASSEMBLY

1. Sew a bright-print small diamond to a white-print small diamond, right sides together. Align the pieces so the overlap meets at the ¼" mark.

   Press toward the darker fabric. Sew another bright-print small diamond to the other end of the white diamond, then press toward the bright fabric to complete a row. Make two identical rows.

   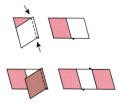

   make 2

2. In the same manner, make a row with two white-print small diamonds and one bright-print small diamond, then press toward the darker fabric.

3. Sew the rows together, with diamonds alternating like a checkerboard. Align so that the seams from each row intersect ¼" from the raw edges. Press seams to one side or open.

   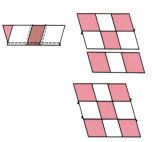

4. Sew on the upper left yellow-print corner to the pieced diamond, right sides facing. Align the flat corner of the triangle with the edge of the pieced diamond as shown. The point of the triangle will extend a bit beyond the ¼" mark for these two pieces. Add the opposite corner in the same manner. Press toward the yellow print.

5. Sew reversed corner triangles to the remaining corners. The raw edges at both ends of the seam will intersect at the ¼" seamline. Press toward the yellow print to complete the block. Block measures 6½" x 8½".

SOLID DIAMOND BLOCK ASSEMBLY

1. Sew on the upper left navy-print corner to the white-print large diamond, right sides facing. Align the flat corner of the triangle with the edge of the large diamond as shown. The point of the triangle will extend a bit beyond the ¼" mark for these two pieces. Add the opposite corner in the same manner. Press toward the navy print.

2. Sew reversed corner triangles to the remaining corners. The raw edges at both ends of the seam will intersect at the ¼" seamline. Press toward the navy print to complete the block. Block measures 6½" × 8½".

BLOCKS NEEDED FOR EXPERIENCE QUILT

6" × 8" Pieced Diamond blocks *make 8 blocks*

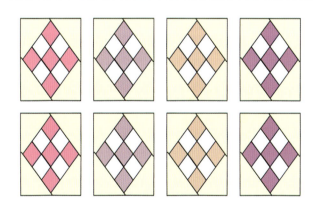

6" × 8" Diamond blocks *make 4 blocks*

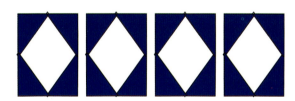

Aging

Threads of Aging

SHORT AND SWEET

You are never too old for a new sewing machine.

JoAnn Belling (age 83)

WHERE DOES THE TIME GO?

As a little girl, I would sit under the quilt being stitched on a frame by my female relatives in Appalachia, watching the light make multicolored patterns against the muslin backing fabric. Quilt making holds a mystique for me. I learned back then that sitting and working on something for hours not only is a valued way to spend time but also can seem to stop time. On many late afternoons, one of the quilters would be surprised to realize that suppertime was approaching. I would hear the question "Where in the world did the time go?" I wanted to experience that magic but did not understand it at the age of seven. I'm only now beginning to understand it in my 70s.

Sandra Sider

Q: What do you think is the biggest challenge confronting quiltmakers today?

I think one issue is that most of the quilters are getting older [*laughs*]. I think the guilds and the quilting establishment need to start reaching out to younger people. I don't know why it is that it appeals to people that are over 50. I think the average age of quilters is something like 58 to 60 or something like that now. I think it would be wonderful if more people, younger women would realize the diversity of opportunity in quilting and how many different things they can do. It can be art. It can be something that decorates your home. It can be something that you sleep under. It's a way of self-expression. It is a way to fill your time. It is a wonderful way to go shopping [*laughs*] to look for fabric. There is so much to it.

Sheila Kramer
interviewed by Karen Musgrave for the Quilt Alliance's Quilters' Save Our Stories (QSOS) project, January 29, 2009
www.qsos.quiltalliance.org/items/show/2579

A QUILTER'S DRINKING GAME

Four of us have been going away for quilting vacations for many years. As we have aged, we have had to adapt a bit. Accommodations with fewer stairs, bringing our own lamps for good lighting, and bed risers to raise tables that were a strain on our aging backs. But we persist and continue to enjoy each other's company as we spend hours laughing and quilting. On one weeklong quilting vacation, I began to notice early on that we were all complaining about our aches and pains a bit too much, so I announced we were going to play a drinking game just like the college kids do. The game was whenever a body part was mentioned, we had to chug water. It didn't take but 10 minutes for us to be laughing hysterically as we chugged our first bottle of water! It's a good thing we decided on water and not an alcoholic beverage, or we would have all been tipsy by 10 a.m. And that would have slowed quilting production down quite a bit!

Jackie Daugherty

YOU ARE HOW OLD?

I have always loved my birthday. I never think of it as getting older, but always as a reason to have fun! The longer I can stretch it out while celebrating, the better, I say! Sometimes that fun has been dinner parties with quilter friends, a travel adventure, or having my family spoil me rotten for the day—usually food related, and hopefully, ice cream is involved. A special joy is watching my husband and daughter make me a heavenly chocolate birthday cake! (My husband does not cook, but he takes instruction well from our daughter.)

One birthday in my NYC studio, my staff and I celebrated with a yummy cake from the shop down the street. Because it was a quilting studio, we were not prepared with knives, plates, etc., so the improv intuition kicked in, and we picked up a 5" × 15" acrylic ruler, and wouldn't you know it, it cuts a birthday cake like a dream!

Several birthdays have been spent celebrating with quilters. In 2019, I started making my plans for a very special getaway with quilty friends to celebrate my 50th birthday in 2020. First I would be visiting a few friends in San Francisco to celebrate with a visit to the Berkeley Art Museum and the

Rosie Lee Tompkins exhibit and a visit to see the darling Freddy Moran. Next, I would be off for two weeks of teaching at Empty Spools Seminars, followed by a week in an AirBnb with my husband in Carmel. Thanks to COVID, that trip did not happen, nor did the teaching, as cruise folks were taken off the ship and quarantined at Asilomar, where I was to be teaching.

The second part of my planned 50th-birthday celebration was a retreat with a few of my closest pals whom I love dearly and who make me laugh till I cry. Well, that also didn't happen. But what I was told by my friends was that since I did not get to celebrate my 50th birthday during the pandemic shutdown at all, that meant I would not be allowed to age until I did celebrate it! So, sadly I have not been able to age, because four years later I still haven't gotten to celebrate the BIG 5-0! Ahhh, it's nice to still be turning 50 for all these years . . . someone please let my gray hair know, and tell menopause to just pass me by . . . I joke as I peel off my sweater, dying from yet another hot flash . . .

Victoria Findlay Wolfe

THE AURA

Although my grandmother's Alzheimer's diagnosis was months away, her memories slipped like grains of sand. Her words drifted between a question and a statement when she said, "You sew." She led me to the stale office in an abandoned section of her house. She was fully present as she zeroed in on a garbage bag. Two jaw-dropping quilt tops sat amid the decades-old, musty fabric inside.

In that electric moment, I learned more about my grandmother than I'd gotten from all our years together. She imbued these works with a palpable life force that transcended her past and present circumstances.

Angelina Holt

HANDS OF TIME

I woke, and in the morning light I raised a hand near my face and thought: "That's Nana's hand."

The hands of my grandmother Florence are vividly dear to me. I don't think of them as "pretty," but beautiful nonetheless as they hugged me, scooped ice cream, and taught me to cross-stitch before I started school. A farmer's wife, Nana had worn hands with gnarled, arthritic knuckles. I see us sitting close together, heads bent over red gingham in a small hoop. Her patient voice coached me but also urged me to "do it right" as I repeatedly aimed for the corners of the woven fabric checks.

Nana drew my attention to quilts when I was in grade school. The two of us would sit on a floral appliqué quilt that covered her bed. Her blue-veined hands smoothed various parts of the quilt as she explained how it was made. A worn fingernail barely tipped up the edges of the pieces so I could see the tiny hand stitches.

Nana's quilts included one that was made from my grandfather's shirts in the softest plaids and stripes. It was a twin-size quilt made just for me, but as I grew up—and my bed grew larger—I refused a top sheet, just so I could sleep directly under that wonderful quilt. I picture Nana's right

hand on the wheel of her treadle machine in her summer kitchen, her left hand carefully guiding the fabric pieces as she treadled.

My great-grandmother Ella lived her last 20 widowed years in the home of Nana and Papa. My mother, Eleanor, often spoke fondly of Ella's fine work as an accomplished seamstress for some of the "society" ladies in our local small town. I readily imagine the precise movements of her hands and her keen eye for style. Ella's hands also lingered long over quilts; the appliqué quilt on which I learned about quilting had been one of hers. My heart warms to know that although I never knew her, our hands and our hearts held the same joys.

My mother took up quilting upon retirement. She'd sit at her sturdy brown Formica kitchen table, hand-cutting and hand-piecing quilt after quilt. Her agile hands were incredibly soft and well manicured. Mom took pride in perfection, and her little cardboard templates and the thin, ultrasharp pencils she used are among my dear possessions. After assembly, her quilts would go to the church basement, where she and several friends would gather and stitch around a quilting frame.

Mom's interest in making quilts came just before the rebirth of quilting as we know it now. My own interest sparked at the same time, and we'd talk for hours about quilting techniques and designs—it was fun to connect, woman to woman, in a shared interest in the last decades of her life; it provided a heartfelt understanding of each other as we each grew a little older. I dream of having hands and a heart as soft and kind as hers.

Aging

I've been a sewist from those cross-stitch days, through a clothes-making obsession during my school years to my current love of quilting. Any thread, fabric, or fiber attracts my interest and always has. I don't remember teaching my two daughters to quilt; it seemed to happen by osmosis—or genetics. Abby loves a modern approach. The spaceship quilt she made for her son will be kept by him forever. Jodi is busy with two daughters of her own, but in precious, guarded moments she works on a delicate English-paper-pieced project. They both embody the desire to carry on the family love of quilting.

The two tiny girls of the latest generation are already showing great appreciation for things handmade. Their tiny fingers delight in using thread, yarn, and cloth in an effort to create. So the generations stitch on—and a family of hands, no matter the size, the age, or the arthritis, keeps busy with needles and threads.

Ann Hammel Murphy

CHAPTER 6

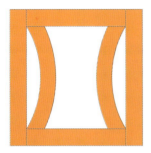

Teaching and Lessons Learned

When I founded my interactive website, www.15minutesplay.com, in 2009, I never imagined that I had anything to offer as a teacher. Even when I was asked to write a book and share my knowledge, I was initially hesitant, wondering what I could possibly teach others. Little did I realize that I had been teaching all along through my website, offering insights on how to build quilts improvisationally, how to use scraps effectively, how to consider color, and how to take risks. Despite this, I was still not comfortable being a public speaker, since I am naturally an introvert and find it difficult to engage with others. The prospect of standing in front of a roomful of people and having their full attention was daunting.

I have since learned some valuable lessons on teaching that have changed my perspective. The first was a piece of advice from my husband, who suggested that I follow the simple formula of "tell them what you will teach them, teach them, and tell them what you taught them." I have found this to be the best advice for preparing how I will teach a new class, and it works like a charm each time! I will add that because different people learn in different ways, it's important to show them as well as tell them. The second lesson I learned was a more embarrassing one: during my first TV appearance, I made the mistake of forgetting to turn off my wireless microphone before taking a bathroom break. Though the entire studio heard me—this was truly a cringeworthy moment—it certainly taught me to always ask where the on/off switch is on any electrical device!

It's exciting to see younger generations take an interest in quilting and carry on the legacy of this art form. As quilters, many of us want to pass on our knowledge and skills to future generations, and it's heartening to see that happening through the enthusiasm of young people.

Teaching can take on many forms that aren't always obvious. I was recently able to meet my pen pal Jade, a young quilter who read one of my books at 14 years old and has been writing to me ever since. It's been a joy to exchange bits of inspiration and advice, and to see her grow in her passion

for quilting. In fact, her love for quilting has already set her on a path toward a career in the field. A gentle nudge toward a new direction is sometimes key in cultivating curiosity and igniting a passion for quilting.

We teach ourselves when we unlearn old habits, ignore old voices, and adapt our processes. Having the confidence to trust our own experiences to make our own rules is our best resource for encouraging productivity.

Have you considered how you share your quilting skills with others? Perhaps taking time to just sit and teach one person rather than a group, if you too feel uncomfortable about "standing in front of a roomful of people." Whether you consider your skills basic or advanced, they are valuable and can be inspiring to others who are interested.

By sharing your quilting knowledge and experience, you can encourage others to explore their own creativity. Who knows? You might even help someone unlock their full potential as a quilter and discover their own unique style. Is anything more valuable than that?

Teaching and Lessons Learned

TEACHING AND LESSONS LEARNED:
Loops & Lines Block

FOR THE 12" BLOCK:

Arcs *orange solid*

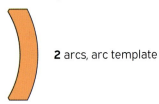

2 arcs, arc template

Borders *orange solid*

2 rectangles 2" × 9½"

2 rectangles 2" × 12½"

Half-Melon Pieces *white solid*

2 half melons, half-melon template

Concave Center *white solid*

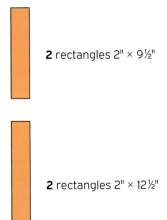

1 center, concave center template

ASSEMBLY

1. Find the center of an arc and a half melon by folding in half and finger-pressing along the edge to mark the center of each curve.

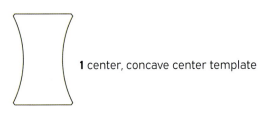

2. Pin centers right sides together, matching raw edges. Place another pin at each end, matching the dog-ears together. Sew this curved seam with the arc piece on top—"floppy toppy"! For curved-seam success, go slowly, keeping the raw edges of both curves together as you sew. Hold pieces at the middle pin, keeping the half-melon piece flat. The fabric bias of the arc piece will then set into that shape evenly as you align the raw edges. Gently press seam allowance toward the arc. Make two of these units.

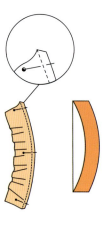

Chapter 6

3. As in step 1, fold the concave center piece and the half-melon/arc units in half to find the centers, finger-pressing to mark. Place one half-melon/arc unit right sides together with the center concave piece, pinning the centers together. Line up the pieces and pin at each end of arc. Sew this seam with the concave center on top—"floppy toppy" again! Gently press seam allowance toward the arc. Repeat with a half-melon/arc unit on the other side of the concave center piece.

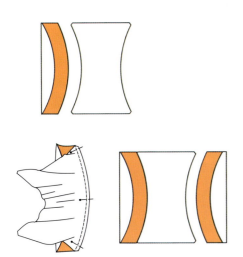

4. Sew a 2" × 9½" rectangle to the top edge of the block, pinning at both ends to align. Press toward the rectangle. Sew the other 2" × 9½" rectangle to the bottom edge of the block, pinning at both ends and pressing toward the rectangle.

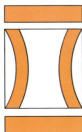

5. Sew a 2" × 12½" rectangle to the right and left sides, pinning at both ends to align. Press toward the rectangles.

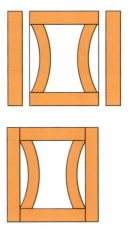

BLOCKS NEEDED FOR EXPERIENCE QUILT

12" Loops & Lines blocks make 6 blocks

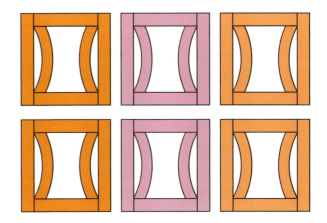

Teaching and Lessons Learned   101

Threads of Teaching and Lessons Learned

MUSCLE MEMORY

Quilting brings me a great deal of teachable moments, sometimes from different and unexpected places. I work as a caregiver with older adults in Maine. Let me share my story about Rita.

I met Rita, a small, strong 90-year-old woman with Alzheimer's disease. She was French Canadian, and she primarily spoke French during our visits. However, language did not hamper our communication.

The history given to me was that when she lived in Canada many years ago, Rita was a seamstress and owned a fabric shop. (I loved to sew quilts and had owned a quilt shop.) Her daughter shared with me that Rita had not sewn in 20-plus years. There was a new sewing machine that had never been used. Rita was the only sewer in the family.

Rita's world was her past. Her actions were restless and her memories searching. Rita would often wander, looking for her parents. One day I pulled out the sewing machine. We sat down at the machine. Within seconds it appeared that this was all second nature to her. The smile proved it.

Our first move was to get familiar with the machine. I removed the needle and was able to evaluate safety for her. It was like riding a bike, like she had never left her machine. I put the needle back in, and we were on our way.

The sound of the machine and two sewers years apart in age came together. I remember her hands, the hands of a sewer, and the movements. The real beauty of this was to witness Rita being back in a space that was comfortable, familiar, and creative. It was like she was home.

In the weeks following, Rita and I worked on making tote bags, pillowcases for her great grandchildren, and a quilt top. It wasn't about the finished products but the process. But the finished items were a gift of Rita to her family.

During our sewing, Rita was calm and present. She shared stories of wedding gowns she had made back in Canada, and she actually opened a drawer that contained records of them. I found something tangible that Rita could connect to. I couldn't help her find her childhood, but I could help her find her meaning.

And I realized it was a two-way street.

Maureen Clark

NOT BOUND BY RULES

I started a quilt top in a modern improv workshop and immediately decided it was going to be for myself. The top was finished by the following night, when it was big enough to comfortably cover me up.

I wanted the rest of the process to be as free form as the piecing. I am a stitcher, always have been, so I decided to hand-quilt the top without a backing, adding only a very thin cotton batting. This, I thought, would allow me to heavily hand-quilt and embroider as much as I dreamt of doing.

It literally took me months to stitch that quilt. I had become quite friendly with it over time, keeping warm under it during the winter months watching Netflix. There are thousands of tiny stitches on that quilt made only by me, X's and circles and itty-bitty dots. I loved every single minute with it.

When it was done, I chose a backing fabric and sent it all off to Shelly at Prairie Moon Quilts to longarm it just enough to hold the three layers together. When it came back to me, it was perfectly soft, as if it had already been washed many times and loved for years. I had missed it so much that I started sleeping under it before it was bound.

This improvisational journey continued to ramble . . . it took about two years before I was finally nudged into binding it.

It's been a few years now, so I think it is finally time to put a label on it!

Michele Muska

LESSON LEARNED

It was important to my mom and Granny that I learn to quilt. So with their tutelage, I did. Mom passed away before Granny, and I wanted to complete one of Mom's UFOs for my nephew's wedding. It was a scrap pattern that she made up—a mix of large white squares and 5" squares on angles, leaving rickrack-type edges.

After worrying and dreading binding those edges, I asked Granny how I could make Mom proud and perfectly bind those edges. Her answer was "Stop worrying about it. Cut those pointy parts off and bind it!" That's what I did!

Shari Brown

STITCHES FOR LOVE

When a newly engaged couple meets with me to officiate their ceremony, I remind them that counseling is required. I use fabric selection as part of the counseling sessions. The bride selects two or three fabrics (in secret). The fabrics are selected based on interests, colors, etc. The groom then does the same. They meet with me and show their fabrics, explaining why each was chosen. (This can turn out to be an interesting conversation between the two, which is the purpose.) Then, using the four or six fabrics, they choose another fabric that ties all the selected fabrics together and represents their life as a couple, explaining the compromises and reasons for the selection.

I often have the mothers (or parents) of both select one or two fabrics as well, also in secret. They give me back the fabrics they have selected and very soon forget about it, as they view it as a counseling exercise, and they have many other details on their minds.

I take the fabrics and select a pattern that works (This can be easy or not! Some fabrics just don't work well together, but somehow they do in the finished quilt) and create a quilt out of the fabrics that all have been selected. I embroider their names and wedding date on the quilt and present it to them at the rehearsal dinner, reminding them of the fabrics and reasons they selected them. It is always such a delight to watch their eyes explode with delight as they point out the fabrics and tell their guests about the fabrics—and they are always *so* surprised that the parents joined in the fun!

Pastor Deena Barwick, PhD

PRESS TOWARD THE DARK

Many years ago, a good friend passed away from breast cancer. We were close friends that crafted together, vacationed together with our kids in tow, and shared life's ups and downs.

When Lisa passed away, she left quite a few unfinished projects, including two partially completed quilt tops for her daughters. I asked her husband if I could take them and finish them for the girls as a remembrance of their mother.

He agreed, and I took them home with all intentions of completing them as quickly as possible. It took me two years before I could begin sewing the patches together. The sadness I felt would be overwhelming, along with the guilt that I needed to finish them. Finally, when I was able to start sewing, it was such a wonderful process of remembering our times together and all that our friendship had meant to me.

One day as I was pressing seams, "Press toward the dark" came to me in a poignant moment. In an instant, the quilter's advice carried more weight—life-altering weight.

What does it mean to press toward the dark—to lean into those places of pain and loss? Life is often filled with bittersweet moments that make the light pieces in our life shine even more.

Three years after my friend's death, I was able to deliver two completed quilts to her daughters. Tears of joy and sadness brought us together in a quilt-wrapped hug. A quilt holds all that and more.

Jackie Daugherty

WHEN LIFE GIVES YOU SCRAPS

As a young mother, I loved making quilts by hand for friends and family members expecting babies. At one point, my husband lost his job, and our family went through a stressful period. During this time, my sister sent me a plaque that read "When Life Gives You Scraps, Make Quilts."

A few years later that sister died of breast cancer, leaving behind three young children. Her husband asked me to make them each a quilt out of her clothes. In an emotional state in the post office mailing off the three quilts, I bumped into an acquaintance. I hadn't realized she was a quilter until, sensing my fragile state, she invited me to a quilt guild meeting. This invite reignited my journey and love/passion for quilting.

Twenty-two years and many quilts later, that plaque still hangs in my sewing space and reminds me every day the comfort, healing, and friendships I have gained over the years by spending the time to take those scraps that life has given me and making them into quilts.

Anne M. Crosby

I'M MARRIED TO WHOM?

I was appraising quilts in Jacksonville, Florida. I always enjoy seeing children's and doll quilts, so I smiled as the lady pulled a crib quilt from her pillowcase. We placed it on the table, and I began filling out forms while my assistant measured and made notes for me. It was a kit quilt from the early '40s, and she informed me it was her husband's baby quilt. I noticed the quilt maker had added one small inner border that was not part of the original kit, perhaps to make it larger.

The lady was pleased with the way the appraisal was done. This was a three-day show, and the next day she arrived with yet another crib quilt, informing me that this one had been her crib quilt. My eyes widened.

"So, the quilt yesterday was your husband's baby quilt?" I asked.
"Yes."
"And this one was your baby quilt?" I confirmed.
"Yes."

I thought long and hard about what to say but finally started laughing. "I'm not sure how to tell you this, but I think you are married to your brother! The same person made both quilts!" This second quilt was also a kit quilt and had that same extra inner border as the first. Thankfully, she had a great sense of humor and laughed with me.

The third day of the show, she returned. "I went home and told my husband what you said. I thought he would fall out of his chair laughing! We looked in the tops of some closets and found the quilt that was actually mine, which is too shabby to have appraised. I just wanted to stop by and ease your mind!"

Teddy Pruett

Teaching and Lessons Learned

Q: Katie, tell me about the quilt you brought today.

This is a quilt that I made with my mother. She originally taught me to sew and do all kinds of handcrafts, but I grew up in Miami [Florida] so we didn't do a lot of quilting. But I did sew clothes and she taught me to knit and crochet and that sort of thing and after she became older and came up here to live in an assisted living [facility] near me, I thought she'd be interested in starting doing some quilting because that's what I had gotten involved in at that point.

And so I took her to the Linus Bee in Black Mountain [North Carolina] and we commenced to make quilts together. And this is a Project Linus pattern, and what I found was the best for her was if we did it paper pieced, which I like to do and she could cut pieces close to the right size with scissors in her assisted living. And then I could do the paper piecing, and we could put it together. And she seemed to get a lot of satisfaction out of that, so this is one of the quilts we made together. She had more fun rearranging the X's and O's, trying to not get two colors together the same but keep the O's and the X's in the right lines and I finally just had to say, "Stop. That's it. That's where it's going to be." Because she kept moving them around and moving them around and moving them around.

Originally it was going to go to Project Linus but I had made her a quilt for her 89th birthday and when she passed away in a rehab facility, someone took the quilt. And when I went to gather her belongings, her quilt was not there, and so I would have liked to keep that as a memory of her but, since that one was gone, I decided that I would ask Sara Hill, who is in charge of the Linus Bee, if I could keep this one because it had special memories of making it with her. So it was sort of my replacement quilt for the one I had made for her.

Katie Winchell
interviewed by Alice Helms for the Quilt Alliance's Quilters' Save Our Stories (QSOS) project, January 26, 2010
www.qsos.quiltalliance.org/items/show/1859

Q: Have you ever had an amusing experience that has occurred from your quilt making or from teaching someone else to quilt? Anything funny?

Well, when I lived in Florida I said, at a meeting, I said, "She who dies with the most fabric wins," and a lady said, "You can't die until you teach me how to quilt," and so I started some quilting lessons, and I had four people. They went beyond my original abilities. They were really good.

Hilda Clemens
interviewed by Carol Clemens for the Quilt Alliance's Quilters' Save Our Stories (QSOS) project, October 10, 2008
www.qsos.quiltalliance.org/items/show/2612

A LYRICAL LESSON

At my job in retail, there is always music playing over the intercom, and one of the guys on our three-member team was always singing along with whatever was on.

One day, the Paul Simon song "Kodachrome" came on, and being from the younger generation, he probably didn't even know what a Kodachrome was, but he was still belting it out for all it's worth.

Singing along normally during the verses, he really took off when it came to the chorus, and when it came to the line "Mama, don't take my Kodachrome away," he belts out at the top of his lungs, "Mama, don't take my motor home away."

My other coworker and I looked at each other as if to inquire, "Did we just hear that correctly?," and began laughing hysterically. We didn't bother to correct him, passing up the teachable moment in favor of a good laugh.

A few days later, the same song came over the intercom again, and I was with my manager and began chuckling to myself all over again about it, so I had to tell her the story, and she got a good laugh out of it too. Now, none of us can hear that song without hearing those *new* lyrics and laughing. In fact, when my manager would hear it come over the intercom, she would call me on the phone just so we could enjoy it together.

My manager and her husband are avid campers, and I had made them a quilt for their RV that had campers on it. After gifting her the quilt, I found out that she was retiring. We had a party for her at work, so I had to make her a pillow with a camper on it, with the words "Mama Don't Take My Motorhome Away" on it, to go with her quilt. The reaction was just what I expected—we've sure gotten a lot of mileage out of that unintentional music lesson.

Katy Kitchen

Q: What did you think about the other quilts that were made?

They were beautiful. Some of them were beautiful. I'm living with some of the girls who also work in Sacred Threads, and they really make a good job. Most of them were not quilters either, like myself, and we were trying to help each other with giving ideas. They would come to me about decisions, and they would say, "Rosa, those stitches looks nice," and I would say, "Well thank you." "Will you teach me how to make them?" And I said, "Well of course, somebody else teach me. Why not?" [*Laughs.*] Yes, we really help each other. That is another thing that I learn here in prison, there is good people around. Even sometimes it is hard being around women all the time, but I mean it is interesting to find out about how they are human beings. How they have struggles just like I had.

Q: If somebody is looking at your quilt, what would you want them to take away? What message do you want?

Hope. There is hope even here when you are down, you can get out of it if you really want to. You have to try. You have to work for it. There is hope.

Rosa Angulo
interviewed by Karen Musgrave for the Quilt Alliance's Quilters' Save Our Stories (QSOS) project, July 20, 2009
www.qsos.quiltalliance.org/items/show/2658

IF WISHES WERE HORSES

Have you heard that old saying "If wishes were horses, then beggars would ride"? I find that particularly apt when I think about the beginning of my quilting journey.

I began with a stack of hand-pieced blocks my mother-in-law kindly gave me when I told her I wanted to learn how to quilt. The blocks had been made in the 1930s or '40s. In the stack were turkey-red and cream-colored Winding Blades blocks, as well as Dresden Plates made from feed sack fabric and hand-embroidered blocks of little bouquets of flowers and assorted star blocks. I was so excited to get started.

If wishes were horses, I would have been far more patient and taken classes before I picked up any of those blocks to make my first quilt. While I may have known the basics of sewing, I did not have a clue about how to make a quilt.

I did get some advice from an experienced quilter before I began my venture into quilting. She told me there were no knots used when making quilts. If wishes were horses, I would have checked that advice rather than just accepting it. Now I know that my first quilt will fall apart if it is ever used.

I read in a magazine that one should practice making small running stitches before embarking on quilting a quilt. Practice? I already knew how to do a running stitch. If wishes were horses, I would have paid far more attention to that advice. Then maybe I would have avoided having those huge stitches smack dab in the center of the quilt that were large enough to catch your toes.

I wanted the quilt to fit my son's bed, so I added large sashing strips and a huge border. The only plus in handling the construction of the quilt that way was that my quilting stitches looked pretty good by the time I got done. But if wishes were horses, I would have learned how to make more blocks instead of adding those huge borders.

I was very proud of my quilt when it was done. When the local quilt guild had their annual show, I offered up my quilt. I stood next to it when I was "white-gloving" at the show. If wishes were horses, all viewers and quilt guild members would be as kind as those I encountered at that show.

After seeing the quilts on display at the show, I knew I had a long way to go and much to learn, but the kindness and encouragement I was offered by the quilting community cemented my love of quilting. If wishes were horses, all new quilters would find that support.

Edie McGinnis

CHAPTER 7

Friendship

You never know when a chance encounter with a fellow quilter will blossom into a beautiful friendship. That's exactly what happened with my "quilt bestie," Shelly Pagliai. In 2009, we connected through a pay-it-forward challenge where participants made quilted gifts for one another. As luck would have it, we both were attending the Houston International Quilt Festival that year, and I seized the opportunity to meet Shelly and deliver her gift in person. She assured me I wouldn't miss her and her Cowboy amid the crowds. And from that moment on, our friendship was sealed!

Over the years, we stayed in touch and supported the start of each other's business. At that time, when I needed longarm assistance for charity quilts, Shelly generously offered to quilt them on her newly acquired machine. We learned together, grew together, and more than hundreds of quilts later have committed to our long friendship. Through countless exhibitions, shows, and ribbons won, we have remained steadfast friends, always on the lookout for ways to inspire and uplift each other.

One funny friendship moment happened when I was scheduled to teach a Double Wedding Ring class at Missouri Star Quilt Co. I was busily setting up the classroom when, to my surprise, my friend Edie waltzed in, followed by Klonda a few moments later, then Shelly, Cathy, and, last, Cheri and Jane. I fumbled over my words, trying to explain that I didn't have time to chat with them. However, after watching me squirm for a few moments, they finally revealed that they had signed up to take my class!

My eyes grew wide as I realized that not only were my friends not leaving, but I would be teaching, correcting, and guiding them. How do you teach your quilting friends without offending their quilting habits, which I knew all too well from our many retreats together?

As happy as I was to share the class with them, I was so nervous. With no time to spare, I asked everyone to gather around at the front to start the class. Edie, always one to lighten the mood, grabbed her chair and dragged it all the way up to where I stood, sitting down with her knees touching mine, and asked, "Close enough?" At that point, I realized that the gloves were off, and I would just teach them as I would any other student.

Klonda, who proclaimed herself "a 50-pinner," ignored my instructions on using only three pins, which resulted in a heap of quiet cursing when she had to rip out her seams. We all laughed a lot, and I was grateful for their support. Teaching your friends your skills for success can be tricky, but a little finesse kept the class focused. We all still laugh about that day. The question "So, how many pins did you use?" never gets old, and it proves that friendship can hold up in what could have been an awkward affair if you all have a really good sense of humor!

Unexpected friendships can bloom anytime, even within one's own family. My niece-in-law, Alice, is a brilliant ER doctor in the UK, and I was elated when her father mentioned that she had caught the "quilting bug." In 2011, Alice and her daughter paid us a visit at our Long Island home. Unfortunately, Hurricane Irene crashed the party, causing an unforeseen delay. Yet, this turned out to be a serendipitous turn of events since it gave Alice and me a chance to sew together and forge an unbreakable bond. While I was writing this book, receiving Alice's story was an affirmation that our sentiments were in sync. Having a family bond that includes quilting is a treasure.

FRIENDSHIP: Bestie Block

FOR THE 4" BLOCK:

Background triangles *blue solid*

 4 triangles, triangle template 4" block (these can be cut from a 2" strip)

Wings *peach print*

 2 trapezoids, trapezoid template 4" block (these can be cut from a 2" strip)

Center *pink solid*

 1 rectangle 1½" × 4½"

FOR THE 6" BLOCK:

Background triangles *blue solid*

 4 triangles, triangle template 6" block (these can be cut from 2¾" strips)

Wings *peach print*

 2 trapezoids, trapezoid template 6" block (these can be cut from 2¾" strips)

Center rectangle *pink solid*

 1 rectangle 2" × 6½"

Chapter 7

ASSEMBLY

1. With right sides together, align diagonal edges of background triangle and trapezoid. Sew the background triangle to one end of the trapezoid; press the seam allowance toward the trapezoid. In the same manner, sew another background triangle to the other end of the trapezoid. Make two matching units.

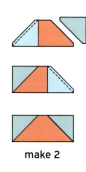

make 2

2. With right sides together, sew a pieced unit to the center rectangle. Press seam allowance toward the center rectangle.

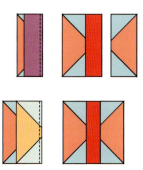

3. Add the other pieced unit to the remaining side of the center rectangle. Press seam allowance toward the center rectangle. Blocks measure 4½" × 4½" and 6½" × 6½".

BLOCKS NEEDED FOR EXPERIENCE QUILT

4" Bestie blocks *make 6 blocks*

6" Bestie blocks *make 6 blocks*

Friendship

Threads of Friendship

COMMON GROUND

I first met Victoria as my uncle's wife. She had a tall, edgy look and was a fine artist. As a doctor from a scientific background, my life was far removed from the art world, and apart from a shared love for my uncle, we had almost nothing in common. I found it challenging to find things to talk about during our interactions.

Several years later, I ordered some premade quilts from a small manufacturer. Upon receiving them, I realized that their construction was relatively simple. As a child, my mother had taught me how to thread a sewing machine, so I decided to try making a quilt myself. I became fascinated by the process and continued to learn through the online quilting community, which was available at any time of the day or night to offer assistance.

The next time I saw Victoria, I discovered that she was a known, excellent quilter, and suddenly we had a significant common interest. While we were caught in a hurricane at V's home on Long Island, she kindly taught me how to paper-piece, which further excited my newfound passion for quilting. Since then, I joined the London Modern Quilt Guild and convinced Victoria to speak to us. She even exhibited at our most significant quilt show in Birmingham. I cherish our interactions and credit quilting for bringing us closer together.

Alice Findlay

FRIENDS WHO SHOP TOGETHER . . .

When I was younger, I would accompany my mom on some of her work trips during the summer. We loved road trips, so whenever she had a lecture, museum exhibit, or work retreat, she'd always see if I could come along. We'd pack up the car with so many suitcases and giant storage bins full of quilts and products to sell that there'd be enough space only for ourselves in the front seats. At the end of a trip, we would know how much we'd sold by the amount of road that was visible in the rearview mirror.

While she was teaching, I'd oversee the product table, handling setup, inventory, tracking tabs, and payments. Doing trip after trip, I'd picked up on the different types of customers who approached the table: The Prepared Shopper, who'd looked everything up online and wanted first dibs. The Peruser, who was conflicted about which fabric to buy because a new line just dropped. The Beginner, who wanted a challenge. The Pro, who already had everything at home. But it wasn't until a trip to Wisconsin that I encountered my new favorite type of customer: the Competitive Friends.

This particular trip, Mom took me with her to Woodland Ridge in Wisconsin for a weeklong retreat of teaching. While I expected most of the vending to occur within the first couple of days, with a quiet last few days of watching over the leftover product, I was in for quite the surprise. As I started tabs for the usual customers who bought items the first day, I was immediately drawn to two women with arms full of kits, fabric, and templates. These two women were friends who had decided to take my mom's class together and wanted the full experience.

Throughout the week, the two women would each sneak away from the other to come back to the table and see what the other's tab totaled, claiming that if the other had spent more than her, it meant she could add more to her own tab. They would laugh and show off their new items to each other like schoolgirls who'd gotten away with something. They quickly became my favorite customers, and I even started whispering numbers to them as they'd walk by the table, tempting them to add more to their tabs. By the end of the week, each had tabs in the hundreds but triumphant smiles at their hauls.

They were so thrilled to have had the week together, and shared in all aspects of their friendship, high-quality time, and shopping time!

Beatrice Findlay

I would like to add that my daughter, Beatrice, and I have taken several road trips across the country to attend quilt events. During one summer, we drove from New York to the South Padre Islands, covering Texas, and although we did not always talk about quilting, the time we spent together while she assisted me in vending (she's great with numbers) provided us with wonderful memories and amusing stories that we will cherish forever. I am grateful that I had the opportunity to demonstrate to my daughter that I could establish a business doing what I enjoy. I have always encouraged her to pursue her passion. Now that she's working her "grown-up job," we don't get to do the road trips that we once did . . . but it doesn't stop us from recalling special memories from those drives.

Victoria

OH, MARY ANN!

We call ourselves the North Fork Quilters. A group of talented women that get together weekly to sew/quilt. Each member has their distinct talents and personality. Mary Ann was a special member. Her quilting was impeccable, and many of her quilts won awards at our local quilt shows. During her younger years she sang opera and appeared on Broadway. She often led our birthday song to friends. Her voice was beautiful, ours . . . not so much! Mary Ann always made us laugh with her stories and the way she lived her life.

On June 8, 2021, sadly, Mary Ann passed away at the young age of 82.

The NFQs had a special memorial for our angel. We spoke of the many funny stories our friend shared or did. One memory that still makes us laugh was when Mary Ann showed us a burn mark on her stomach. We each had a puzzled look, wondering how she managed to do that. Nude ironing was the cause, and she accidentally brushed against the hot iron. . . . Oh, Mary Ann! Before our memorial evening ended, we all gave a special toast to our loving friend with a shot of Fireball Whisky (one of her favorite drinks). That sure did shake some heads! LOL!

Before Mary Ann passed, she made sure that her daughters knew what to do with all of her quilting supplies. Mary Ann knew that her daughters would not want any of them, and feared they would be thrown out. They loved her finished projects but had no interest in sewing. About a week after Mary Ann passed, I received a phone call (as did a few other members) from her daughter, asking if we would clean out her sewing room and make sure that all her supplies went to her mother's special quilting friends, North Fork Quilters, and Eastern Long Island Quilters' Guild. Of course, we agreed, and off we went to Mary Ann's home.

Oh, the things we learned about our beautiful friend! She was organized, but boy did she have material! It was hidden all over her home. We even found material stored in her bathroom vanity! There were many uncompleted projects she had on her design wall ready to be sewn. Oh, and underneath that project was another quilt she designed but never finished. And yes, underneath that project were two more projects. . . . Oh, Mary Ann! So many tears were shed during this process, but there was laughter too. Everyone had a Mary Ann story!

Mary Ann's wish was granted. Supplies and material were shared. There isn't a day that goes by that one of the NFQs or a member of the ELIQG doesn't think of Mary Ann. It could be her special seam ripper, a pair of scissors, a ruler, or using some of her beautiful quilt fabric.

Our friend's projects that were never completed are slowly getting sewn together. Her finished projects are being donated to charities for others to love. We miss our friend, but she shines a special light through everything she has given.

Missing my beautiful friend.

Karen Nicholson

STITCHED TOGETHER

When I moved from NYC to Vermont in 1987, I mailed requests to my family and friends for a scrap of fabric to make a quilt. The move was exciting but also had moments of deep sadness and loneliness. Receiving letters and cards that included a scrap with a brief explanation of why it was chosen helped me stay connected.

In order to remain financially stable, I took on work as a seamstress for a maternity bathing-suit company. One day as I was sewing crotches for the suits, I announced that I had taken a test and discovered I was pregnant with my first child! I am still amused that I happened to be sewing crotches—I'm silly that way.

I stayed on for a while until it was time to rest and nest. That's when I worked the most on my "Shoofly, Don't Bother Me" quilt. Each shoofly was made using the fabrics folks sent. I finished it the year my second child was born (I think), as it took time to hand-quilt. I entered it into the Vermont Quilt Festival that year. It didn't win a ribbon, but I was still proud to have it be my first quilt ever to enter.

The year my third child was born, my best friend from NYC and I decided we'd start an exchange of Drunkard's Path blocks. We chose a bright yellow as the constant color. We also decided to make two copies of each block, one to send and one to keep. We hand-stitched them all and will hand-quilt once final decisions are made. We started in 1992, and it is now 2023. We finished the blocks many years ago, but not the quilts . . . yet. Our layouts reflect our personalities. Both so good, both so different.

Kate Pietschman

RENEWED

In 2004, I was diagnosed with breast cancer. My sister routinely attended my clinical visits. One day, she asked, "Is there anything you regret in life?" I answered, "Yes, selling my baby quilt in a yard sale." In 1990, we had moved to Maine, and I added that tattered quilt to the auction. I was unable to fix the moth-eaten, frayed-edge cloth. A neighbor immediately bought it for three dollars, as she was an avid quilt maker.

We never talked of that conversation again. It was just a moment my sister and I shared in a quiet, tense waiting room.

I was a year beyond my illness, and life had returned to a normal pace. Surprisingly, a box arrived at Christmas. I opened it to find my baby quilt. Nothing had changed. My sister had found the neighbor, told my story, and rescued the quilt that had never been repaired. I melted in tears.

Until one day I told this tale at a reunion in Cape Cod, Massachusetts. My classmate Laurie, a professional quilter, whispered, "Let me restore this for you." So once again, a box appeared, with my pristinely renewed patchwork inside.

I consider this a part of my cancer journey, a simple question only a sister would ask and of a 50-year friendship that healed my soul.

This 63-year-old quilt now comforts my grandchildren when they cry from an injury or are chilled from the mountain air. Its resting place is on a white wicker rocker, at our cabin in the woods.

Amy Henkes

Q: Tell me about your interest in quilting.

We had a group quilt meeting today. It is a group of eleven really dynamic women. Ann Horton and I started the group, we are not exactly sure when, we think it was about in 1991. So the group has been going quite a long time and it has been really relatively stable in terms of the membership over the last probably seven years. I think that all of us in the group would acknowledge that secondary to the group, our quilting skills have grown immensely. We meet regularly and we really push each other. We critique each other; there is a lot of different quilting styles within the group so it helps you stretch in a different direction. I think more importantly—you saw that little quilt we have been working on—is who we are as people and how the group has come together as a support group. We know each other pretty well and pretty intimately at this point in time, and the quilts were the avenue to move into those relationships with these wonderful women. That is kind of a big piece of quilting for me.

Joyce Paterson
interviewed by Karen Musgrave for the Quilt Alliance's Quilters' Save Our Stories (QSOS) project, March 9, 2007
www.qsos.quiltalliance.org/items/show/1549

THE FABRIC OF FRIENDS

"The Fabric of Friends." That was the name I gave to a quilt I entered in my guild's quilt show. I needed a name fast, the entry deadline was quickly approaching, and that name popped into my head, so "The Fabric of Friends" it was. What I didn't know then, but my subconscious did, and what I have recognized since, is that name truly told the story of the quilt, its concept, design, and construction, and the story of a friendship that goes back over 60 years.

In August 2013, nine women gathered at a log cabin on Lake Barnum in the woods of northern Minnesota. We were all Minnesotans at one time. We were there to celebrate an amazing friendship—friends since nursery school for some, friends since grade school and junior high school for others. The group came together as the years went on. And as more years went by, not surprisingly, changes came to pass. Life happened. There have been glorious successes—adventures, careers, marriages, children, and grandchildren. There have been frightening and tragic times—divorces, serious illnesses, and deaths. The broad spectrum of life experiences is deeply represented in the long history of this group.

So back to the Minnesota north woods and a quilt. I wanted to make a quilt to commemorate this event. How to represent the event? How to get my friends on board to help in the making of it? Fabric shopping, of course! Front Porch Quilt Shop in Walker, Minnesota, was just a few miles from the cabin and perfectly met our needs. I had brought a focus fabric with me. I laid it out on the cutting table, and it guided all nine of us as we scoured the shop, everyone searching for a fabric she loved. Selections were made, fabrics were cut, and, for a group in which eight out of the nine women were not quilters, the choices came together in a beautiful and remarkably cohesive way. There was lots of laughter and no second guesses. The quilt was on its way!

The retreat ended, but my work was just beginning. After a bit of a search, I found a pattern that captured the essence of our story: Minnesota roots and colorful personalities, reflected in each person's chosen fabric, brought together in a quilt—pieced, sandwiched, stitched, and bound—much in the way that love and decades of experiences build a treasured friendship.

The quilt design includes nine stars. Minnesota is the North Star State. There are nine flying geese blocks. Loons, woodpeckers, bald eagles, and many other species of birds had joined us, and Canada geese were everywhere. Several pine tree blocks form a north woods landscape, and log cabin blocks represent our shared home at the retreat. As luck would have it, each log cabin has nine "logs." Everyone's fabric was pieced into the quilt. Each person was woven into the creation of this friendship.

Quilts can get worn and raveled, torn, patched and repaired, even discarded. Friendships can suffer over time. This friendship is no different. Feelings have been bruised, hearts have been broken, and bonds have been sorely tested. Our quilt, "The Fabric of Friends," remains as intended, a commemoration of a north woods retreat celebrating a remarkable friendship that spans more than 60 years.

A quilt and a friendship. Comfort and joy . . . I am grateful.

Lolly Schiffman

FRIENDSHIP REPURPOSED

In 2007, the United States Air Force replaced their Woodland and Desert camouflage-patterned uniforms with the new Airman Battle Uniform (ABU), designed to be worn in all environments. As a result, I found myself with a boxful of outdated uniforms when I was preparing for a military move. Remembering that Victoria, whom I had known since seventh grade, had become a successful quilter, I reached out to her for help. We had shared classes and extracurricular activities in high school and had reconnected on Facebook.

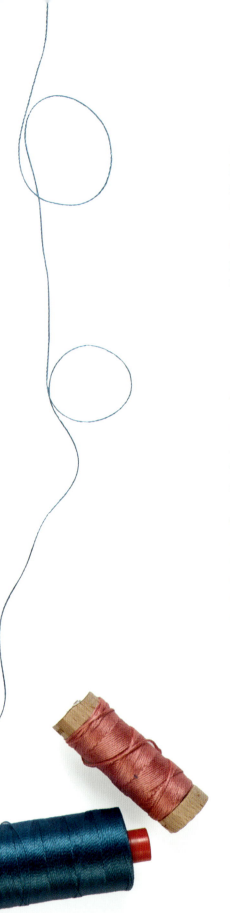

I gave Victoria full creative control, as I had no specific vision for what the quilt should look like. The result was breathtaking. The quilt was made from pieces of uniform that had served me in various military stations, including Whiteman Air Force Base, Missouri; Royal Air Force Lakenheath, United Kingdom; Ali Al Salem Air Base, Qatar; and Sather Air Base, Iraq.

I retired from the Air Force in 2013, and I'm grateful for the idea of a quilt as a way to repurpose the old uniforms instead of disposing of them. The quilt now holds a special place in my heart as a reminder of my service to my country.

Bob Waldorf

ASK AND YOU SHALL RECEIVE!

Many years ago, I was approaching my 40th birthday and decided I'd like to celebrate it with a quilt made by my friends. I thought I'd ask just a few friends and maybe get nine blocks for a wall hanging. I designed an appliqué block and made small kits with fabric and detailed instructions for each block.

When word got out that I was doing this, many friends were actually offended that I didn't ask them to make a block. I didn't realize how many good friends I had! I received 32 blocks! One woman, who previously did only needlepoint, learned to appliqué so that she could finish a block for me. I was so overwhelmed that I put the blocks away for almost 20 years. I finally decided to finish the quilt for my 60th birthday. When it was finished, I entered it in a quilt show and won a ribbon!

Stephanie Braskey

CHAPTER 8

Travel

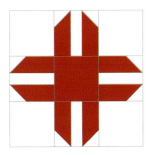

I've always been someone who enjoys the freedom of being on the move, both in my creative pursuits and life in general. Traveling allows me to experience moments that I simply can't find anywhere else. These moments bring me just as much joy as the process of making a quilt.

I've often heard people say, "I can't wait to see what this trip inspires in you!" But it's not just travel that inspires me. Sometimes, taking a break from sewing and going for an afternoon walk can generate new ideas. Stepping away from the project for a while can help clear my mind and let fresh inspiration in.

Driving is another way I find inspiration. I've taken many road trips that have led to new quilt designs and patterns. And even while flying, I've come up with some of my best ideas. Once, I even wrote an entire book on an airplane!

During road trips with my daughter when she was younger, I gained a valuable perspective. As we sang along to music or played games, my daughter would interrupt and ask, "Mom, can I think now?" She would then proceed to share the most creative and imaginative stories. It was a powerful reminder that inspiration can be found in the simplest of activities.

Sometimes, my travels have directly inspired a quilt, while other times I've pulled fabrics reflecting on impressions of a trip to make a quilt. And like many of us, I've purchased fabrics on my trips that have become the basis for a new quilt. My travel-inspired quilts include some about the droughts in Botswana and the language of trees from watching elephants in Africa. I even finished hand-quilting a small quilt in Antarctica while snow pounded down around me.

Venturing into the unknown can be a powerful tool for me to generate fresh ideas and expand my creative horizons. Whether it's traveling, trying a new hobby, or simply engaging with different perspectives, exposing myself to new places can help break down mental barriers and spark innovative thinking. A fresh mind brings fresh ideas!

And speaking of the unknown, have you ever found yourself in a random corner of the world, running into people you know and never expected to see there? It's crazy how small the world can feel sometimes!

I once ran into quilter Linda Teufel from Ohio on a mountain in Japan while walking to see the snow monkeys! And in Samarkand, Uzbekistan, I ran into quilter Karin Hellaby from the UK. These remarkable encounters make traveling even more exciting and create memories that last a lifetime. I will always remember them because of those moments!

You just never know where you'll meet a fellow quilter. Maybe at the grocery store, or on a plane, or even in a remote mountain town. Wherever I go, I'm always on the lookout for the next opportunity to connect with other quilters and share our passion for this beautiful art form.

How has stepping away from your usual surroundings inspired something new?

The next time you're feeling stuck in a creative rut or in need of some inspiration, why not pack your bags and hit the road? Who knows where your travels will take you and who you'll meet along the way!

Travel

TRAVEL: Transit Block

FOR THE 9" BLOCK:

Main print *red print*

 1 square 3½" × 3½"

 8 rectangles 1⅝" × 3½"

Background *white print*

 4 squares 3½" × 3½"

 4 rectangles 1¼" × 3½"

 8 small squares 1⅝" × 1⅝"

FOR THE 12" BLOCK:

Main print *pink print*

 1 square 4½" × 4½"

 8 rectangles 2" × 4½"

Background *white print*

 4 squares 4½" × 4½"

 4 rectangles 1½" × 4½"

 8 small squares 2" × 2"

ASSEMBLY

1. Draw a line diagonally from corner to corner on the backside of the white-print background small squares. Lay a square on top of main print rectangle, with drawn line going from lower left to upper right, right sides together. Stitch on drawn line. Trim ¼" outside the stitching line. Press toward the main print. Make 4 left units. In the same manner, make 4 right units with the drawn line going from upper left corner to bottom right.

2. Sew a left unit to the left side of the center rectangle. Press toward the left unit. Sew right unit to the right side of the center rectangle and press toward the right unit. Make 4 pieced squares.

3. Lay out the pieced squares and cut squares as shown. Sew into rows, pressing seams in alternate directions for each row. Sew rows together to complete the Transit block. Blocks measure 9½" × 9½" and 12½" × 12½".

 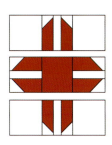 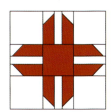

BLOCKS NEEDED FOR EXPERIENCE QUILT

9" Transit blocks *make 6 blocks*

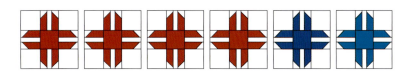

12" Transit blocks *make 6 blocks*

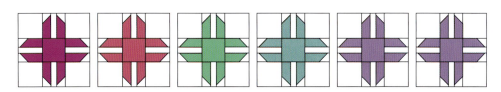

EXTRA BITS NEEDED FOR EXPERIENCE QUILT

2 squares 3½" × 3½". A great opportunity to fussy cut from a multicolor print!

Threads of Travel

TOKYO QUILT FESTIVAL

One of my fondest memories of traveling was when I taught master quilters how to sew curves on sewing machines in Japan. As I entered the room with my interpreter, I was met with a group of neat and tidy, quiet women who listened intently. I'm used to cracking jokes during my lectures, but I wasn't sure how they would translate. It took awhile for me to warm up, and they were initially hesitant to use their English. But as we laughed and encouraged each other, the atmosphere in the room became more relaxed.

During the demo, a group of five or six strangers came in and stood at the back of the room, watching us. I leaned over to my translator to ask who they were, and she blushed with embarrassment as she told me that they had heard I was tall and had come to see for themselves. We all laughed and had a good time together.

Later, when I taught at the Tokyo Quilt Festival, I faced another challenge. My sewing station was set up on a platform with a desk that I couldn't fit my legs under, no matter how high we raised it. So, I had to teach and sew "side saddle," which amused everyone and provided more laughter.

The best part of exhibiting in Japan was that I was going home ahead of my quilts, which left me with a very large, empty, suitcase! We made several trips around Tokyo's fabric town section, and the quilt show, so we had no problem tipping the scale at its maximum allowed weight for our flight.

The weather in January added to the excitement. We had rainy and snowy days, an earthquake that made the Tokyo Dome hotel sway on the 32nd floor, and a delay in our return due to snowstorms in New York, which gave us two extra days to play. We even had a sunny 75-degree day, which resulted in me getting sunburned.

The Tokyo Dome hotel also had a shopping mall attached, with a giant rollercoaster that my assistant Kim and I couldn't resist riding. But our trip to the shopping mall and bath spa took a hilarious turn when I was turned away for having tattoos. A sign outside the spa read "No tattoos allowed," and we were told that only members of the Yakuza had tattoos. We still laugh about that to this day. People are often surprised to learn that I'm a professional quilter, rather than a member of the Japanese mafia!

Victoria Findlay Wolfe

FABRIC ON THE MOVE

As usual, I had ordered fabric eight to ten months ahead for my quilt store. At the beginning of the pandemic lockdowns, I started thinking, "How will I connect to my customers and sell all that fabric?" No quilt shows, no quilting classes, nothing . . .

I always wanted to go on holiday in a motor home / RV, but my husband was never interested.

So I thought, "What if I packed my shop into a rented motor home and went to different cities in Sweden where they have a quilt guild?" I don't know who was happier, me driving off in a fully fabric-packed RV or my husband standing at our house waving me away!

What a great way to meet customers! We could have only two or three people inside (Swedish COVID restrictions), so everybody else stood outside chatting. Each person came out, telling the others what they bought, like a small show-and-tell. "Oh, I want that fabric too" was often heard outside . . . and in they came again for a second round.

One question I got at every stop as customers looked around the RV was "Where do you sleep?" There was a bunk bed filled with a long line of fabric bolts. Every night I needed to move all those bolts away to clear my bed to sleep. And of course my bed had a quilt on top!

A lot of ladies have their own RV, and the first thing they said coming in was "Well, this is how I want our RV to look, quilt stuff on every shelf. I wonder what my husband will say?"

I have made this trip once a year for three years. I'm out on the road for two weeks, and it's really a mini vacation. Meeting customers all over Sweden who normally don't go to shows, giving them an opportunity to pet fabric . . . what a joy!

My husband still refuses to go with me though . . . he doesn't know what he's missing!

Maria Bussler

TRAVELING WITH JULIA

We called her "Mommy" until her last breath at age 84. Julia was larger than life: outspoken artist, belly dancer, flashy dresser, and, according to my childhood diary, a big grouch. At age 67, I now understand what made her grouchy in my youth . . . me! Julia dabbled in all art mediums, and in the 1970s her focus was on fiber art and quilting. She took one quilting class and established herself as the premier local quilting instructor. She had no interest in old-lady quilting . . . no cardboard templates or measurements necessary! As a smarty-pants college student, I thought her venture into quilting was ridiculous. I mean, who on earth would have the time and patience to quilt? True to form, by the time I started quilting she had moved on to something else.

As a 49-year-old, I was an avid quilter and the mother of three adolescent children. I was both exhausted and perhaps grouchy in the eyes of my children. But in my eyes, Mommy was no longer grouchy; she turned out okay. When she asked me if I would accompany her on a trip to Thailand, her treat, I said, "Yes," without hesitation.

Exiting the plane in Bangkok, I was overcome by the aroma of burning crops, incense, cooking smells, and other unidentifiable smells, both sweet and putrid. At this time, I was not a world traveler, and I was a good but safe quilter. Instantly I became intoxicated by the sights, sounds, and smells. As we walked by the spirit houses, temples, shrines, monks, and flower markets, my only thoughts were "Wow." Oh, and the colors took my breath away . . . saffron and red became my new favorite color combo. Color, pattern, and texture were duly recorded in my many photographs. I was overflowing with design inspiration.

Returning home, I was excited to start my Thailand-inspired quilt. I decided to do an interpretation of the Tree of Life symbol. I drew my freezer paper pattern full size and appliquéd these shapes onto an ombre saffron background. I embellished the quilt with hand quilting, hand embroidery, beading, and shisha mirrors.

I completed "The Tree of Life" seven years later and am very proud of it. This trip was a big step in becoming more observant of the world, boosted my creativity, and launched me on a lifetime of travel. I am grateful to my mother for starting me on this path. Julia was a great travel companion on several more trips; positive, fun, never grouchy. However, she was always late to the bus, which embarrassed me just as she had done when I was a teenager. Some things never change.

Allison Lockwood

A QUILT STORY

My mother and I were driving across the country in the summer of 1975. I was going to college in California, and this was an opportunity for some relaxed mother/son bonding before I started to make my own way in life. We went from our home in New York through Ohio and eventually made our way to Nebraska, where both my mother and father were born and raised. I'm not sure where it was that we saw an antique store and decided to stop—Nebraska is a very long state, and we had relatives in many different towns—but we were drawn to this shop. Mom liked fabric and buttons and antiques with character; she quilted clothes and Christmas ornaments; she had made quilts for me, Bob, and Cathy . . . but she wasn't yet a quilt collector. That would come later.

I liked vintage clothes and was looking in a closet in the back of the shop when I saw a quilt folded up on the floor, looking sort of lonely and forgotten. I picked it up and brought it to the front to show my mother. We recognized it as a crazy quilt, and there was something about it that was energizing—the colors, the whimsy, the aging silk. I asked how much it was, and when I heard the shop owner say, "Five dollars," I decided it was meant to be.

I gave this quilt to my mother for being such a wonderful traveler, and it hung in the stairwell of our Chappaqua, New York, house for years until it was replaced by a higher-quality version. Mom gave it back to me, with love and many memories. I've always believed that that quilt found me and played a meaningful role in sparking in my mother a lifetime of quilt collecting. Carolyn Ducey, the Ardis B. James curator at the International Quilt Museum, wrote this on the occasion of the 25th anniversary of the gift of the James Collection to the University of Nebraska: "In 1979, they [my parents] selected a quilt they liked at a local antique sale, then added another the next year, and then three, then five." That's when they became collectors.

But a few years before that, my mother "acquired" her first quilt. It might not have been the prettiest quilt, or the best made . . . but it was the first.

Ralph James

CUSTOMS SCARE

Before my first international trip for an exhibit and teaching, I had heard horror stories from other quilters about customs officials damaging or confiscating their quilts due to unclear documentation. I was nervous about flying to Australia and how customs would handle my quilts, but I made sure to have all the necessary paperwork and exhibition documentation in order. When I arrived and collected my suitcases at baggage claim, I approached the customs agent with trepidation. He asked me about my reason for visiting and what I had in my bags. I explained that I was a quilt teacher and had an exhibition. To my surprise, he simply replied, "Ah, just a quilter, go ahead . . ."

I picked my jaw up off the floor and made a beeline with my astonished eyes to the exit, feeling both grateful and a little indignant at the same time.

I mean, let's be real, when is it ever okay to hear someone say, "just a quilter"? But in this case, those words were music to my ears and a sign that my quilts were going to make it safely to their destination.

Victoria Findlay Wolfe

CORONA-CATION STORY QUILT

In February 2020, we flew to California with plans to embark on a cruise to Hawaii with our friends. It was the kind of adventurous trip to a tropical location that one dreams of being able to experience. That dream came to a halt on the afternoon of March 5, when the captain unexpectedly requested everyone to return to their cabins for isolation until we arrived in San Francisco on March 7. It was discovered that passengers / crew members on the prior cruise had recently tested positive for COVID-19.

We were assured that our meals would be brought to our rooms and that any updates would be provided as they became available. Thank goodness I had brought along hand appliqué, as one cannot live on TV alone! I was hand-appliquéing a large Princess Feather block—which, ironically, has a similar look to the COVID-19 photos we were seeing on TV! I even connected with a fellow passenger who had brought her small Bernina and projects for the sea days—little did she know how handy it would be! For an additional two days, we continued to sail in a circular pattern off the coast of San Francisco.

Social media was a wonderful gift, since it was our only link to the "world." Quilters, friends, and family messaged us, comparing news and offering support. On March 11, we finally were able to disembark and were flown to Dobbins Air Reserve Base in Marietta, Georgia, for a 14-day quarantine.

Over the course of the following days and weeks, we were interviewed by West and East Coast TV news stations and newspaper and magazine journalists. It really was a frenzy—I had to keep a calendar of when the interviews were happening, but it made the days go by quickly!

Following the Georgia quarantine, we would continue our quarantine for another week in our home.

Remember the saying "When life give you lemons, make lemonade"? I didn't know that this would be so true till we started receiving our mail. Unbeknown to us, Kay Butler of Denton, Maryland, and Didi Salvatierra of Hendersonville, North Carolina, took it upon themselves to ask friends to make appliqué hearts for us. When our mail finally arrived was when we found out that hearts from all over the country were being created and mailed to us, even a block made by my 91-year-old mother! Over the next several months, I created my first story quilt that highlights many of the events, the good and the bad. What a wonderful surprise those blocks were, and how heartwarming to know that so many friends had been praying for us!

Karen Dever

WELL-TRAVELED FABRICS

Traveling adds a whole other dimension to quilting. I made so many friends on my quilt trips I took many years ago, and some that I am still in touch with. I have many fond and funny memories . . . not to mention fabulous fabrics I brought back home. I can still name the fabric and the place I bought it! Oh, the random information our heads hold! Useless? I think not!

I recall once coming home from Hawaii when my luggage was lost. I was so upset! All I worried about was that the lovely floral fabric I bought in Hawaii might be lost forever. What a relief when my bag was recovered, and I could create something beautiful from that fabric.

I had the best time ever searching for fabrics on trips that I might not ever find at home. Isn't it amazing what powerful memories a random piece of fabric can hold! Bon voyage!

Helen Beall

> *Q: You are a professional truck driver
> [. . .] and you are a quilter. You do the majority of
> the quilting in your truck. [. . .] Would you tell us
> about that please?*

It's a confined little area, but it's a nice little work space that has allowed me to—instead of just going to the back and reading books, as I was doing before, or going into truck stops and not necessarily enjoying the company inside the truck stops—has allowed me to seek out other activities, fabric shops. But specifically, piecing and doing quilting in the truck all by machine. Eighteen months ago, if you had told me that I could do this in the truck, I would probably have looked at you skeptically. But with the suggestion from my wife, because she was running out of book stores and the Goodwill to go to to find me things to read, she made the comment, "You know, maybe you ought to try this." The journey started in July of '09. It started with a quilt, I didn't get to show it to you on the truck, but it's called "My Guy" and it was a very simple design. We cut the pieces out and put it into little baggies. She put a sewing machine, an old Singer sewing machine, on the truck. Three weeks later I came home and had it all pieced together and done. So it was a self-taught lesson at the same time. Her comment to me then was "I've created a monster." Of course after that, every time I would go home, we would go to—we've got about two or three little fabric shops there in Colorado Springs we go to. The ladies have gotten to know me well enough that I have to show and tell. They are always looking: "What did you bring us this time?"

David White
interviewed by Jeanne Wright for the Quilt Alliance's Quilters' Save Our Stories (QSOS) project, September 15, 2010
www.qsos.quiltalliance.org/items/show/2128

Q: Tell me about the barn quilt project.

The [Barn Quilt Trail] project [. . .] was an idea, a concept, that probably was birthed about the same time that I watched my grandmothers quilt and when we would go visit them in the Roane County, West Virginia. During road trips with Mother and Dad, my mother created a car game to keep my brother and I quiet. Since we grew up in West Virginia you can't play the typical license plate car game when you're traveling on the back roads of West Virginia, because all you saw was West Virginia license plates. So Mother created a car game and we counted barns. If it was a certain kind of barn, you got two points; if it was another kind of barn, you got three points; if it had outdoor advertising on, you got a bonus of ten points if you could read it. Barns like "Chew Mail Pouch" or "See Rock City" or "RC Cola," all kinds of outdoor advertisements. Red barns were higher points. The game led to discussions and questions about the barns; Were they an English barn, were they Welsh, German?

And what the purpose of the barns was. It became a history and cultural opportunity for my mother to engage my brother and I, and my father too, in conversational teaching moments, whether I knew it or not, and they were exciting. I looked forward to seeing barns. And then as a teenager, we traveled through Pennsylvania, where I was first introduced to the German, Pennsylvania Dutch barns with their hex signs, which had the most colorful, wonderful, geometric designs on them, and they were worth fifty points in our car game and that was pretty exciting. [. . .]

This project, the Quilt Trail development, I believe has really brought more focus on quilts and barns, too, just equally. Barns are, hopefully, the barns will be preserved. They're in more danger

Travel

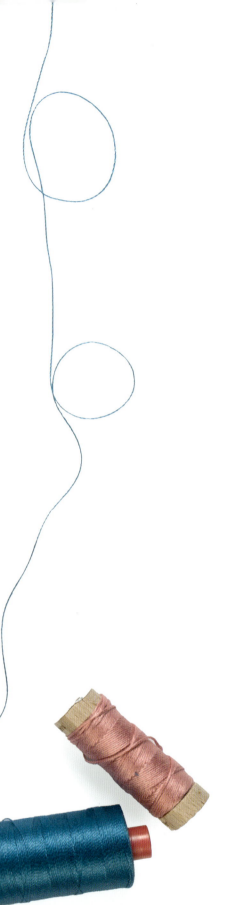

than the quilts are of disappearing, I think, because the quilts have a little more protection. But from the beginning, part of my dream for this whole project was that not only would we use quilt squares in a public venue on our barns to celebrate who we are and to create economic opportunity, but also I had hoped that we would be able to preserve those stories, about those that built the barns and the family farm stories and the quilts. Of equal importance are the quilts in those families and the stories that go along with them. Because preserving those stories and hearing and listening to them, will help us to know where we came from and who we came from. We can reflect on the strength that it took too—and energy and focus and dedication and hardship, all of those things that our foremothers and forefathers did so we could be where we are today. And we need to remember those stories. We need to celebrate who they were because that's our DNA; maybe our larger community DNA connects us all together just like a quilt.

Donna Sue Groves
interviewed by Karen Musgrave for the Quilt Alliance's Quilters' Save Our Stories (QSOS) project, June 18, 2008
www.qsos.quiltalliance.org/items/show/2656

CHAPTER 9

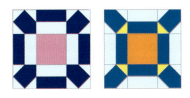 # Remembering and Grief

As we know, grief can be a challenging and overwhelming experience. It can be a difficult and emotional process to navigate, taking time to heal and come to terms with the loss. It's also true that grief can lead us toward gratitude, as we reflect on the positive experiences and memories that we shared.

Using quilting as a therapeutic way to process grief and create something meaningful and tangible to honor the memory of a loved one or past experience is one way to work through it. Quilting allows us to stitch together memories and emotions, creating a physical representation of them. As we work on a quilt, we can reflect on our feelings to help us find some peace.

The finished quilt can become a time capsule, preserving an event and incorporating the thoughts, feelings, and nostalgia of the past. It can serve as a visible reminder of the love, joy, and connection we shared with the person or experience, helping us feel grateful for the time we had together.

When I was asked in my QSOS story for the Quilt Alliance in 2011 if I had ever made a quilt to get through a difficult time, I said no. However, over the years since, I have discovered quilt making as an outlet to express my grief. One such quilt I made is called "Raw Emotion." I created it the day I found out through social media that someone I was once engaged to had died suddenly. The confusion and pain of that moment led me to quickly cut double-knit polyester fabrics and throw them frantically on the wall, using bold colors to represent my emotions. I then spent a more controlled, calming time later to hand-quilt the pieces together. The design and making of the quilt happened as fast as throwing a baseball, while completing it was like the sound of the ball hitting the glove. The quilt is a treasure of emotions that comforts my head and heart when I look at it.

With needle in hand and fabric at my fingertips, I settled in on a journey of emotional healing. Each stitch and every piece of cloth became a tangible representation of the thoughts and feelings that I was struggling to process. As the quilt slowly took shape, I began to see the beauty in my pain, the strength in my vulnerability.

Now, as I look upon the finished quilt, I am filled with gratitude for this physical example of my emotional journey. It serves as a testament to the transformative power of creativity, and a reminder that every quilt holds within it a story waiting to be told. It reminds me to consider the legacy that I am leaving behind, and the impact that my life has had on those around me.

For me, this quilt is not just a collection of fabric and thread; it is a symbol of my resilience, a testament to my strength, and a tribute to the human experience. And as I wrap myself in its warmth and comfort, I am reminded that there is beauty in every struggle, and that the journey toward healing can be as beautiful as the destination itself.

If you have a memory or emotion that you still need to process, quilting can be a powerful way to express and release it.

 REMEMBERING AND GRIEF: Facets Block

TIP: With a few differences in color placement, two variations of this block are created.

FOR THE 6" BLOCK:

Background *white print*

 4 rectangles, rectangle template 6" block

 4 triangles, triangle A template 6" block

 8 triangles, triangle B template 6" block

Rectangles *blue print*

 4 rectangles, rectangle template 6" block

 4 pointed rectangles, pointed rectangle template 6" block

Center *bright print*

 1 square, square template 6" block

FOR THE 9" BLOCK:

Background *white print*

 4 rectangles, rectangle template 9" block

 4 triangles, triangle A template 9" block (*For 9" Facets variation, cut these triangles in a contrasting color.)

or

 8 triangles, triangle B template 9" block

Rectangles *blue print*

 4 rectangles, rectangle template 9" block

 4 pointed rectangles, pointed-rectangle template 9" block

Center *bright print*

 1 square, square template 9" block

ASSEMBLY

1. Sew a triangle A to the end of each pointed rectangle. The triangle is dog-eared to make it easy to align with the rectangle. Press seam allowance toward the triangle.

2. Sew a triangle B to each of the other two straight sides of the pointed rectangles. These triangles are also dog-eared to easily align. The dog-ear points on the triangle B are also the start and end of the seam. Press seam allowances toward the rectangle.

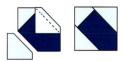

3. Sew a white background and blue-print rectangle together along the long side. Press toward the darker rectangle. Repeat to make 4 of these units.

4. Arrange the pointed-rectangle and rectangle units around the center square as shown. Rotating the pointed-rectangle and rectangle units creates a second block version. Sew the units together in rows for Facets or Facets Variation, then sew the rows together to complete the block. Press seam allowances following arrows on diagrams.

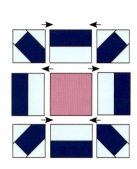

Facets

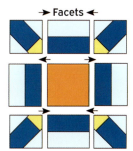

Facets Variation

BLOCKS NEEDED FOR EXPERIENCE QUILT

6" Facets blocks *make 4 blocks*

9" Facets blocks *make 6 blocks*

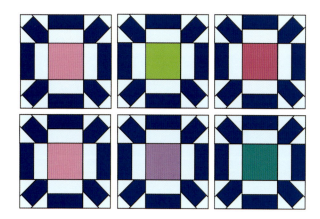

9" Facets Variation blocks *make 2 blocks*

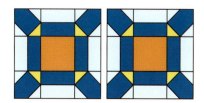

Remembering and Grief

Threads of Remembering and Grief

FARM GIRL

During my college years, I took a creative-writing class and studied Native American culture with a Lakota Sioux professor. He was a wise and respected teacher, and I admired his reverence for tradition.

One day, the professor came to class and shared sadly that his wife's father had passed away. As part of our class, he asked us to attend the ceremony that evening. When I arrived, I was struck by the solemn beauty of the scene. The deceased was laid out in a simple pine box, enveloped in a beautiful morning star quilt.

That evening, we honored and celebrated the peaceful body. I sat with his family and other students, taking it all in. It was my first time seeing a body that was not embalmed, so it was very different from my own upbringing, but it was also quite beautiful and natural, which felt so strangely perfect.

As I sat at the ceremony, I couldn't help but think about my own mortality. I wondered what kind of quilt could I make, that would one day hold and cradle my body. This was a celebration of life so unlike the services I had been to, and I knew this was becoming a pivotal moment in my life.

Many years later, I was still thinking about that moment, and I started to gather my thoughts and fabrics, waiting for the right pieces to fall into place. I made several attempts, piecing together fabrics into stars from my own clothes, from my family's, and even from my friends'. While each step got me close to the idea, the visual never quite described who I am. I would stash the quilt top and its pieces away in a box, only to pull it out year after year, to examine it, cut it again and again, trying to make it "just right."

Another year or so later, while I was working on my first double-wedding-ring series, I pulled those star pieces back out, put them up on my wall, and added parts of double wedding rings into the corners, and my quilt "Farm Girl" finally fell into place. To this day, it is the quilt I have asked my family to bury me in, in a plain pine box.

Victoria Findlay Wolfe

BOLD EXPRESSIONS

Sally and I became pals shortly after I started making quilts. She was a very experienced quilt maker from Arkansas and new to Seattle. At a quilt guild meeting, she invited me to be in a group for making "out of the box" quilts. She named the group "the Rebels." We studied old African American

quilts and other quirky utility quilts, from the collections of Eli Leon, Scott Heffley, Roderick Kiracofe, and Corrine Riley, along with the quilts made by the residents of Gee's Bend, Alabama.

Early on, we realized we couldn't get the spirit of these quilts with modern fabrics. We needed to make them from old clothes, like the original makers had done. Sally and I would go to the Goodwill on 99-cent day and come out with 20 to 30 men's shirts. Nothing gave us more joy than finding those gorgeous checks, stripes, and plaids in the men's shirts aisles. We'd come home and cut them apart, saving the buttons, cuffs, collars, and seams. We wound the seams into colorful balls and filled our glass vases with buttons. We loved our new fabric selection!

Sally lived alone, and her house was completely devoted to quilting. Her kitchen drawers were filled with thread and other sewing notions. We'd get together at either her house or mine about twice a month. We'd egg each other on to try new things that would bring life and originality to our quilts. Our goal was often to use more outlandish fabrics, or to choose a crazy combination of prints, plaids, and stripes. We wanted our quilts to have the charm and brilliance of the old utility quilts. We were good at giving each other courage to do something we would never have done alone.

One day, she came to my house for an afternoon of sewing. I'd been working on some blocks inspired by a quilt I'd seen at Corrine Riley's quilt exhibition. I liked my blocks well enough, but I just wasn't feeling the energy and excitement of making it. I thought Sally would say, "It's good. Keep going." Not so!

She took one look at my design wall and said, "You know, LeeAnn, you don't bomb out that often." I was so thankful! It was exactly what I was thinking, but I didn't know what to do about it. She said, "Let's sew these blocks together in strips and cut them apart. Now go get your outrageous fabrics and we'll sew it all together."

Remembering and Grief

The next few hours were a wild and fun afternoon of fast sewing, not thinking. We grabbed whatever was in front of us and sewed it all together, as fast as we could, adding random scraps when needed to make the strips fit. At the end of the day, the quilt top was finished. It's my most favorite ever.

It's an extremely special and fortunate gift to have a friend who sees something in you that you may not see in yourself, someone who is honest with you about your work and tells you when you could do better. Now that Sally's gone, I feel the lack of that "partner in crime." Sometimes, in my sewing room, I'll say, "Okay, Sally, help me out here." And, if I can get my head out of the way, I do sense her nudge to try a certain fabric. It usually turns out that fabric is one she had set aside and labeled for me before she passed away.

LeeAnn Decker

MEMORY QUILTS—CONNECTING TO THE OTHER SIDE

It was a headline in the Sunday paper: "3 Local Brothers Killed in Terrible Accident."

And just like that, the young boys were gone, never to grow up. Their three sisters remained—they had stayed home that day and now found themselves lost in fathomless grief.

This tragedy led me into that intersection of love and pain, where quilts can give tangible, immediate comfort to those left behind. I felt utterly compelled to make memorial quilts for the sisters, even though I hardly knew the family, just through school.

But I had to offer to make them.

I wrote to the family right away, offering to make a quilt for each sister out of their brothers' clothes. I said that in one year or ten, I would be honored to do this, if ever they were ready to make this decision.

To my great surprise, I got a call that same week. The very next day their mom, plus her own mother, myself, and a grief counselor, went through every shelf, closet, and drawer, emptying them of shirts, T-shirts, jeans, shorts, pants, ties, sports uniforms, and pajamas. They went into bags that I loaded into my car.

The three quilts, all twin sized, took me the next three months to make. What I hadn't known was that those quilts were for *me*.

Forty years before, on the shore of Lake Michigan, a five-year-old boy slipped away from all the moms and kids enjoying a day at the beach. This was the 1950s; there were a lot of kids, and his absence went unnoticed. He was a daredevil by nature and ran into the big waves all by himself!

And he never came back. I was four when my brother Freddie drowned. This catastrophe shattered my family as it was, with one nightmare after another sucking us under just like those waves. Divorce, alcoholism, suicide—there were no grief counselors back then, no support groups.

My mother never mentioned Freddie's name again; that was how she dealt with it, along with having another baby immediately. Thank God my sister was born ten months later, right before my parents split up. We struggled forward into our lives as if he had never been. His memory became faint, and then disappeared from me altogether into our family's chaos. After all, I was barely four when Freddie had left us.

Halfway through cutting up one of the boy's shirts, removing collar and cuffs, I became frozen, with the scissors forgotten in my hand as I stared into the past. I was doing all this to honor and grieve Freddie.

How much I would have loved to have a quilt of the clothes he had worn all those decades ago. I could wrap up in his memory, fold it all around me, and continue to love him. I was making the boys' quilts so their sisters could have that.

The family has since moved away, and I can only hope that those quilts have brought the girls comfort. I hope they have helped transmute their loss into loving, living memory.

After the quilts had been delivered, I thought I was done grieving my long-lost brother. But not quite . . . a few years later I was finishing up a quilt about the cottage where we had spent our summers on Lake Michigan, an embroidered landscape that took me six months. The very last thing to go on that quilt was not even planned; it just happened: I embroidered Freddie's name in the sand by the shore.

Then I was done. His sweet memory is alive in me forever.

Allie Aller

UNFINISHED

When I was 12, I became aware that my mother had become a quilter. The evidence lay in small pieces of thin fabric appearing in alarming quantities in her bedroom, where I was not allowed. Her door was never locked, so I had taken advantage of her absence one afternoon to find out what she was up to. She was a mother that needed to be watched.

I carefully held her little squares in my small hands and knew there was no way I'd be able to replicate such precision. There was nothing my mother couldn't make: Jelly rolls, afghans, spoon dollies, pinafores, stained-glass windows . . . even a dollhouse out of a gun cabinet. She played the accordion and piano too. I admired her hands and hoped someday I would have ones just like hers. Thick veined and strong.

Days later, her 1977 Singer sewing machine appeared, and larger squares that had been created by sewing together the little ones lay on her bed and formed a pattern that was completely unfamiliar to me. I stared hard at the mystical design and wondered what it could possibly mean. Had she joined a cult?

She was a woman of contradictions: if something seemed impossible, she found a way to make it possible—a sometimes dangerous fearlessness that she wove into me as well. It threads its way through both the best and worst parts of my life.

The one big difference was her willingness to confront "the machine." That big hunk of metal intimidated the crap out of me. It was loud, fast, and sharp, with a piercing needle that could rip right through the tip of your finger. Intimidating. Hard. With rules. My fear of the machine later drove me to rebellion against rules of all kinds. Just like my mother.

I don't know why, but she never attached the binding. Never completed it to lay it on her bed, my bed, my sister's bed, or anyone's for that matter. Instead, the beautiful series of squares went into a box one day and never came out again. It just disappeared.

Over 40 years later, I saw some quilts for sale on the side of the road in Idyllwild, California, where my partner and I had bought a home. I became obsessed with them. I bought one. I urged my sister to buy one. Then I went back with my husband and bought another. Big, beautiful, finished quilts.

About a year later, when we decided to sell that house, I left my quilts behind. I still don't know why. Perhaps they were a part of an unactualized dream, and it hurt too much to bring them along. Perhaps I felt I had to abandon them in order to move on from that part of my life. I told myself someone else needed them more than I did.

The needle had caught me with its piercing sting after all, leaving behind pain that (like my mother) I needed to bury away, unfinished.

Cady McClain

AND THAT IS ALL THAT MATTERS

I'm a very visual person, and I love creating my aesthetic and finding my voice through color, fabric, and pattern. I'm inspired by the deep connection I feel to the centuries of tradition that came before me, especially when I'm hand-quilting or tying a quilt. I take pride in making things that are both utilitarian and beautiful that provide warmth on both levels.

Sadly, I learned that my quilts would provide the same warmth and comfort for my sweet mama during the last few months of her life. She had a stroke on April 6 and was actually doing pretty well despite being airlifted to the hospital in Iowa City. She had a week of steady progress and a very optimistic recovery prognosis from her whole team. She was supposed to be transferred to acute rehab for two weeks before going home but then tested positive for COVID upon discharge.

During that first month in Iowa City, I was able to see her for hours almost every day, which we both desperately needed. As soon as she left the ICU on day 3, I was pretty much permanently lying in bed with her: spooning her, holding her hand, rubbing her back, making sure she knew I was right there with her and that she was safe. I took a quilt with me; I knew she would be cold, plus I wanted her to have something cheerful to look at and that would make her feel wrapped up in a hug from me. I had a steady quilt rotation and changed them every week to give her a different view.

Once she moved into a nursing home in my hometown on May 5, she continued to suffer from complete exhaustion, which had a detrimental effect on her appetite, which had a detrimental effect on her energy. We got stuck in that never-ending cycle, and things got scary way too many times.

She started hospice May 27, and it was a slow, sad waiting game. The uncertainty was terrifying.

In the beginning of July, I started to think she was winding down. I truly hoped it would be over soon for her sake. I'd never seen such an exhausted human being. I knew it was the best thing for her, but that didn't stop the internal protest, "I don't want my mom to die!" It was all just so incredibly heartbreaking.

After getting a call from the hospice nurse that she was vomiting, I raced to her side. I guess I somehow knew, because I packed clothes for a couple of weeks instead of a couple of days. I got off work until the following weekend, so I was able to be with her almost constantly her last week. She got progressively weaker and stopped eating or really talking.

When I arrived the morning of July 19, my aunt Beth was there with her. After I crawled under the quilts to spoon with Mom, Beth told me she was going to go take care of a few things and come back in an hour or two. As soon as the door closed, I immediately burst into tears and held my mom so tight while I sobbed. When I finally tried to calm down, I started taking really deep inhales, and on the exhales I whispered, "I love you, I love you, I love you, I love you, I love you . . ." That went on for about a half an hour while her breathing got quieter and quieter and then finally stopped. My sweet, darling mama died peacefully in my arms, and we were alone just like I wanted it to be, holding her so she felt safe and loved until she reached the other side.

Everything after that is a blur, but I stayed at her apartment until I drove home for work that weekend. I went back on Sunday night to clear out her entire apartment and turn over the keys on Thursday. When I finally got in my car to drive home late that afternoon, it hit me so hard that I'd never be able to go home again. And that no one would ever love me as much as my mom did. I still cry pretty much every single morning when I wake up, and it hits me that I'll never get to see my mom or talk to her or hug her again, at least not in this plane of existence. And while I'm looking forward to when that's not my first devastating thought each day, I also know that that, too, will hold some sadness. This pain and heartache is still a strong connection keeping us tethered. Although this was one of the hardest experiences I think I'll ever go through, it was the greatest honor of my life to be there with her and to be there for her. I can't imagine being anywhere else.

I saved a boxful of her clothes that I'll make into a quilt for me someday soonish. And then I'll get to be the one wrapped up in a hug from her. She was just the most amazing mom, and I will never stop missing her.

Ellen Ruden

REMEMBERING

Oh, the memories . . . the older we get, the more memories we make to remember. Sometimes, those we love don't travel along with us as we get older, and all we have are the memories they left us with when we were younger.

My mother passed away in 1969. I was only six years old at the time, so I don't have a lot of memories of her. Her mother stepped in to raise me and my siblings, so my grandmother ended up being more of a mother to me than a grandmother.

She's the one who started me sewing when I was eight years old. It was her sister-in-law, my great-aunt Charlotte, who sent her a big garbage bag full of fabric scraps to give to me. I can clearly recall sitting in my grandmother's breezeway, sifting through the bag, hardly believing it was all for me, and imagining the possibilities!

I think that's the day I became a true quilter.

I was 12 years old then, and I immediately started a quilt from the scraps in that bag. The pattern I chose? A Seven Sisters quilt. The reason I chose it? My mother had made one, and it now belongs to my brother. I wanted to make one too, in honor of her. It made me feel more connected to her somehow. And making it from the fabrics in Great-Aunt Charlotte's scrap bag helped connect me to her.

My grandmother was a quilter too, and we ended up doing a lot of quilting together. She was so proud of her Giant Dahlia quilt that won an award in a local show. A few years later, I made a quilt that won a contest, and she was equally proud of me. After that, I entered another show but didn't win anything, and I showed her the judge's sheet. She read it, and said, "Well, you just don't have to tell anyone about that!" After I stopped laughing, I informed her that the judge's comments are there to help you improve your future quilting.

I always wanted her to see a major show with me, but by the time I started attending some of those, she could no longer do that much walking. When she finally stopped making quilts herself, she instead helped me with some of mine: matching up pieces for me to feed through the machine, threading needles for me as I whipped down bindings, and looking through books and magazines together. She passed away in 2000, but I know she'd still be just as proud of me today. I'd love for her to see some of the quilts I've made since then.

I never finished that Seven Sisters quilt, and I'm not even sure what happened to that UFO, but I still have some of the fabrics from that big garbage bag in my stash of scraps, and I use some of them every now and then. It keeps the memories alive, and connected to the women in my family who have passed on. Memories of my mother, my grandmother, Great-Aunt Charlotte . . . and of my own quilting journey. Looking back, I wish I had finished that Seven Sisters quilt, but I'm sure, as a first attempt, it's probably best that I got rid of it! Maybe I'll start another one, now that I know what I'm doing. You know, just to keep me connected to those wonderful ladies.

Shelly Pagliai

THE LIFE OF A NINE-PATCH QUILT

I have never been a prolific quilt maker, so it is a bit surprising, even to me, that quilts and quilting are such an important part of my professional and personal life. My first was a simple nine-patch, and I was about nine years old. My mom's cast-iron Kenmore was tucked into a corner with windows on both sides in her bedroom. I remember the light it brought into the room, and the sky seemed so big from that corner. It offered a beautiful view of our backyard hill and my dad's garden that sat on top. Sewing for hours on end in that corner by myself was sometimes the only peace I had from dealing with a very stressful sibling.

When I started the quilt, I randomly pulled scraps from the large handmade African basket next to the sewing machine, a gift from my cousin Glenn from his time in the Peace Corps in Africa. Fabric pieces from the clothes and hats my mom made for herself and me filled it. I am not sure who prompted me to start a quilt, maybe one of my aunts in Maine or my 4-H leader? My mom made only curtains and clothes at that time. I cut and sewed the nine patches together, not paying much attention to the type of fabric I chose, just the print and color. I knew I needed something for the sashing, so I found some amazing cheddar fabric and zigzagged it to the blocks.

Somehow I knew it needed a filling, and I pulled the lavender plaid flannel sheet from my bed. My mom found me an old sheet for the backing. So resourceful even as a young child, I was very determined to finish it. That quilt was at the end of my bed until I went to college, and it came with me there too. I was on one side of the cinder-block room in a twin bed with my quilt folded at the end. My life-size poster of Jimi Hendrix with his baby-blue guitar next to me. While my roommate had a poster of Holly Hobbie with a matching spread . . . such an unlikely pair we were.

Then that quilt went to Boston with me for 10 years and was used as a picnic and beach blanket for me, my husband, and friends. I never was careful with it; it was meant to be a useful companion. What I remember the most about this quilt, besides the time I took to make it, was that it became the blanket I put down in our backyard on the grass for my babies to sit upon. As each one was able to sit up on their own, I would get them outside on that quilt. I can still picture it now, those sweet boys on that ill-made quilt. I have to say it makes me cry to think about what it meant to me to make it. The circumstances I made it under and how sewing it took me away to a peaceful place in my own home. It was much loved by this point and a little worse for the wear. I occasionally come upon it when I am cleaning out a closet and know I would never toss it, so it is still here somewhere.

Michele Muska

ALL THE LUCK IN THE WORLD

My mother passed away from complications caused by Alzheimer's disease.

Several years after her death, I made a small quilt as a way to tell her story. It's small, 25" × 35", but, for me, it describes her journey into dementia perfectly.

When dementia starts, there are just little "slips," nothing major, and if the person is quirky anyway like my mother was, you don't always notice them. As time passes, of course, the "slips" become worse, and at the end there is very little you can see of the person that was. The body is still there, but the person you knew is gone. I believe that person is still buried way down deep inside, but it can no longer get through the disease.

My mother was always encouraging. When my first husband was lost at sea, I was in my mid-20s. My parents lived close to the University of New Mexico and told me that if I would finish my degree, they would give me room and board so I could devote all my time to study. I finished an MBA. Every time I went to a test, she would see me off at the door and tell me, "All the luck in the world!" Every time. Later, as dementia became noticeable and progressed, I didn't grieve the change. Nor did I grieve when she died in 1996. I had remarried and had a rich professional life. But as I got older (I'm 75 now), I missed my mother. I missed "All the luck in the world!" And I regretted not spending more time with her.

I made "OJ's Quilt" in her favorite colors. Made 20 years after she died, it has deep, rich colors at the beginning with just a little "quirk" or two of taupe. And then the taupe grows across the quilt as the dementia progresses, until at the very end there is just a tiny bit of that deep, rich color that I associate with my mother. It was a way of saying, "Thank you!," and a way of saying, "I'm sorry I wasn't there for you more!," and a way of saying, "You mattered!," and probably most importantly, a way of saying, "I love you!" It was an outlet for a grief I had never expressed.

Ann Magetteri

Q: Did quiltmaking help you in getting through that period of time [divorce]?

I was pretty engrossed in quiltmaking before my husband and I separated. I'm not sure that it was related at all to the divorce. I've used quiltmaking on multiple occasions to deal with strong emotions.

My very first art quilt was about the death of my dog. He died and two years later I was working on my master's degree in counseling. I took a grief class and we were required to do a project. I was still having dreams about that dog. It was almost as if he was my first born and he had died. He came before I had children because I had my children later in life. The puppy and the dog were when I was in my 20s. [. . .] Even years after he died, I was still dreaming that I was visiting him and I would wake up sad and crying again. Then I thought, it's just a dog. You need to get over this.

In the grief class, I learned how grief can be complicated. There can be different issues affecting your grief process. Sometimes working on something that's a tribute or a memory to your lost person in your life can really help. I took photos of my dog that I had from my collection and I put them in a little art quilt. I put his collar on it, his tags. I saved a scrap of his hair. He had long hair and was a Lhasa Apso dog and a really cute little guy. The process of making that quilt actually helped me work through the grief. I stopped having the bad dreams of missing him. It was really therapeutic.

Kathy York

interviewed by Peggy Camp for the Quilt Alliance's Quilters' Save Our Stories (QSOS) project, November 4, 2011

www.qsos.quiltalliance.org/items/show/2264

I SEE DEAD PEOPLE

In the film *The Sixth Sense*, nine-year-old Cole tells his psychologist, "I see dead people." In a way, I see them too.

Early in graduate school I encountered the material culture theory of Jules Prown. He claimed that the *mind* of makers was embedded in the material objects they made. Applying his theory to quilt research, I encountered real people—not disembodied minds—situated in time, place, and circumstance, connected in a web of relationships, and whose quilt making provided a desperately needed sense of wholeness or expression.

I came to know Rose Kretsinger of Emporia, Kansas, through her small collection of near-perfect quilts. She completed her final work, "Paradise Garden," in 1946. Rose designed its appliquéd medallion, bursting with abundance, as a widow, living alone, and her only son away fighting the enemy in Europe. She poured into it every ounce of her professional artistic training and needle skills. As I studied Rose and her quilts, I met a woman whose anxious heart yearned for the soothing joy of beauty and bloomed with creative energy.

I carefully documented 120 of the 400 quilts Nebraskan Ernest Haight produced in his lifetime. After college, he had aspired to be an engineer, but duty required that he manage his aging parents' dairy farm instead. In 1927, he lost his first wife in childbirth, and then the economic collapse of the Great Depression threatened his new family. In these tragic circumstances, Ernest began to quilt. He drafted intricate geometric quilts, more like an engineer's drawing of machine parts than quilt blocks, and precisely pieced them from vibrant cotton solids. Everyone he knew received a quilt for graduation, their wedding, or the arrival of a child. By studying his quilts, I came to see that quilts were the glue in his life: he kept his sanity by creating, communicated the importance of his family and community through generosity, and demonstrated resilience by using the means under his control.

Lucinda Ward Honstain of Brooklyn, New York, endured a troubled marriage, deceitful husband, and public humiliation. Yet, I found appliquéd into her now-famous "Reconciliation Quilt" from 1867 a defiance to her circumstances and declaration of freedom from her abuser. It explodes with exuberant folk images and scenes from New York City life: an organ grinder, a washerwoman, a clam salesman, and a Black man declaring his freedom from enslavers.

And there is Raymond Fry, whose embroidered name and the year *1918* appear on one of the oddest redwork coverlets I have seen. The white background is punctured with crudely stitched outlines of American World War I-era propaganda juxtaposed with angels guiding guileless children through mortal danger. Raymond was a man whose naively rendered religious and nationalist images reveal an intriguing and puzzling identity. Raymond is long dead, as are Rose, Ernest, and Lucinda. Yet, I *see* them. I even care for them, because I found their minds, souls, and storied humanity traced in their quilts.

Jonathan Gregory

CHAPTER 10

Food

Food is a delightful source of inspiration and connection! As I teach my quilting retreats, whether in my New York City home or in faraway places, I always make sure to gather my students around the table for a delicious meal. It's during these moments of shared culinary joy that the process of quilting transforms into a bonding experience like no other. In fact, I find that these mealtimes are just as valuable as the quilt lessons themselves! There's nothing quite like a group of quilters crowded around a table, swapping stories about their sewing origins, discussing the colors and patterns that inspire them, and regaling each other with tales of how their love for sewing has intersected with their lives in unexpected ways.

And let's not forget the ice cream parties! As much as I adore quilting and traveling, my love for ice cream knows no bounds. I've been known to throw a few ice cream parties for my students, whether at the end of a five-day workshop or simply because the day demanded it. But it's not just about the ice cream. Food is a central part of my family's joy. My daughter and I share a passion for hot and spicy cuisine. Some of our most memorable travels have been based entirely on the food we wanted to taste, with India topping our list for its mouthwatering, spicy dishes.

During the pandemic lockdown, when I wasn't busy cutting and filling orders from 5:30 a.m. to 9 p.m. each day, I found solace in the kitchen. I cooked my way through an Indian cookbook, then moved on to Korean cuisine. It was through my love for quilting that I met some incredible artists from Seoul, including Mingi and his mother, Hong Joo. Thanks to Instagram, I was able to connect with them, along with a few of their friends who later traveled to New York to visit my shop.

When I finally had the chance to visit South Korea, I knew I had to learn more about the cuisine. I planned to sign up for a Korean cooking class in Seoul, eager to get hands-on experience making kimchi. But what happened next was even more special. Hong Joo, Mingi, and his sister Higi took

me to Hong Joo's father's forest and the home where she grew up. I met her mother, brother, uncles, and cousins, the entire extended family, and for a moment I felt like I was a part of their family. It was a magical experience that etched a spot in my heart. And as a bonus, I got an authentic lesson on how to make a fast batch of fresh kimchi from Hong Joo.

Food memories are powerful for me. I still have a recipe for soup that was given to me while teaching in South Texas that has become a family favorite. And I fondly recall driving to southern Minnesota to visit my grandparents as a child. My grandmother Elda, who was the quilter in our family, also happened to be an excellent baker. She always had a repurposed gallon ice cream bucket filled with sugar cookies waiting for me. I can still taste those cookies paired with Blue Bunny vanilla ice cream, and I looked forward to Christmas, when she would make us fried bread dough dipped in sugar!

Whether it's through shared meals, recipe sharing, or even quilts inspired by food, the connection between food and quilting is undeniable. Both provide opportunities for creativity, community, and storytelling, making them a perfect match.

So, do you have any fun traditions with your quilter friends centered on a shared meal? Have you ever made a quilt inspired by food? Do you sew at your kitchen table, only to have to clear it off each time you need to cook a meal?

FOOD: Dimensions Block

FOR THE 12" BLOCK:

Sides *four different prints*

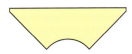 1 side each from 4 prints, side template

Circle *solid cream*

 1 circle, circle template

ASSEMBLY

1. Find centers on curved edges: Fold each side piece in half and lightly press with an iron to mark the curve center. Fold the circle in quarters and press lightly with an iron to mark.

   Unfold circle and fold each quarter section together to mark the eighths with a small finger press.

   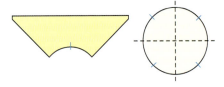

2. Sew side pieces together along diagonal edges to create a square with a hole in the middle. Press the seams to one side.

   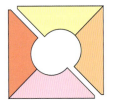

3. Line up the circle fold marks with the seams and centers on the open square. Place a pin at each of these points, with the floppy square piece on top. Sew around the circle, pausing to adjust the fabric fullness for each eighth and keeping the raw edges of both curves together as you sew, As you sew from pin to pin, keep light pressure at the next pin, so the circle piece will stay flat and the fabric bias of the side piece will then set into that shape evenly as you align the raw edges.

4. Press seams away from circle. Block measures 12½" × 12½".

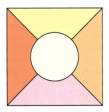

BLOCKS NEEDED FOR EXPERIENCE QUILT

12" Dimensions blocks *make 2 blocks*

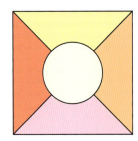 

158   Chapter 10

Threads of Food

Q: How many hours a week do you quilt?

That is hard to say. I tried keeping track. [. . .] I don't keep track of my quilting because I do it whenever I can. [. . .] We live in a town house and so I kind of have stuff in every room and I do a lot of moving around. I cut downstairs in the kitchen and I sew in the guest room if I'm quilting, but I piece in the master bedroom where the smaller sewing machine is. I'm all over the house. I tend to do something, stir the soup and then walk over and do something related to quilting. I do it as much as I possibly can.

Sheila Kramer
interviewed by Karen Musgrave for the Quilt Alliance's Quilters' Save Our Stories (QSOS) project, January 29, 2009
www.qsos.quiltalliance.org/items/show/2579

THERE ARE NO CALORIES AT QUILT CLASS

Before I was a quilter I was a chef. There are more things in common between the two than one can imagine. The colors, the textures, the variety in styles and trends. Eating and enjoying food is a universal experience, and our mood and sensibilities can often be reflected in the food we choose. It's the same when we quilt; our choices are guided by our experience, necessity, and emotions.

Like in cooking, my favorite part of quilting is the cutting, as well as sharing the finished product with family and friends. Sharing recipes, meals, and baked goods among like-minded quilty peeps adds to the sensory experience when we sew together.

I always try to bake for my classes; we are mostly middle-aged women taking time out from otherwise hectic lives. A hot cuppa and a piece of homemade cake with my quilting friends can turn the most terrible of days around. Over the years I've also tried to combat the guilt that some of my quilting students have with taking a day off for themselves, giving themselves permission to do something that they enjoy. That guilt can often extend to food, so we joke that there are no calories at quilt class.

I'm not sure if it's the same for every teacher, but I find that one of my most valuable skills is listening. Not everyone comes to learn how to quilt; for many it's a brief escape from their demanding family life, a stressful job, or even loneliness.

With all this quilting and eating happening, it's amazing that I've never had anything spilled on a quilt. Maybe that's because other quilters appreciate the effort and time that it takes to finish a quilt? With my family it's a different story—quilts are put away for the rowdy parties; they know that Nutella and quilts don't mix. There are family quilts, quilts for cuddling and picnics, and then there are the show quilts, the ones sitting by the lounge waiting for binding. We don't eat near those, yet!

The love of quilting and food has guided most of my holiday choices over the past few years. New and old friends share travel stories, quilt shops, and restaurants to visit. We swap notes on where to go for the best coffee and cake. I'll often arrange to meet internet quilters in a café. Once we've placed our order, we chat for hours, pulling out our phones to look at quilting photos, photos of the kids, or a great restaurant recommendation!

Both food and quilting are important to me. Sometimes we are hungry for excitement and adventure, looking to try new things. Sometimes we just want something comfortable and fast, an easy make to soothe frazzled nerves. The repetition of a familiar pattern or recipe to keep our souls fed through a rough patch. The important thing to remember is that both have merit, the tricky showstopping quilts and the everyday warmth from something simple. They each have their place in our creative and culinary journey.

Lorena Uriarte

THE LEGACY QUILT

It all started with an article in the *Washington Post* food section, not about food but a quilt: the Legacy Quilt. The handmade quilt was on exhibit in New York City to represent the contributions of African Americans to American cuisine. One of the members in my quilting minigroup had read the article and shared the information with us about the Legacy Quilt. We all had the same reaction: interest in learning about this intersection of food and quilting as an expression of celebration and respect. I planned on being in New York City in June for a quilt retreat, and the group knew my plans. The chorus of "You have to go" was loud and clear. I extended my stay and made arrangements to see this quilt at the Africa Center.

I was on a quilty high after my three-day retreat but was equally excited to take in the exhibit. When I entered the center, I immediately saw the quilt; it hung on the wall directly facing the entrance. The quilt is large, 14 feet tall and nearly 30 feet wide. It is composed of 406 blocks, each one telling a story that deserves recognition. I learned that the Museum of Food and Drink (MOFAD) originally decided to use a quilt as the vehicle to educate the community because quilting has a deep connection in African American culture. The Harlem Needle Arts (HNA) organization was commissioned by MOFAD to tell over 400 years of history about the contribution of African Americans to food and drink in a quilt through designing, constructing, and providing information about blocks.

There was seating in front of the quilt that others and myself took advantage of. While I sat there, I met students, artists, quilters, foodies, and historians who, like me, were exploring the quilt, using our phones and the QR code to link the stories to the block. We picked out our favorite blocks by block design, geographic location, time period, or occupation. We smiled, cried, and were humbled by the enormity of the exhibit.

I presented my Legacy Quilt program to the minigroup with pictures and commentary. There was a moment of silence, then a rush of ideas as to how we could honor the quilt and the quilt makers. Deborah volunteered to research more on the legacy of Black quilt makers and present a program at a local quilt store. Another class being planned is celebrating the rich history of African quilts and textiles. For the foodies among us, I shared the MOFAD list of cookbooks by African American chefs, with the promise to share our favorite recipes. Karey, who in her day job is director of food services in a major hotel chain, told her chefs in the NYC area about the exhibit and encouraged them to go. The feedback she received was overwhelming with the recognition of these contributions. What a rich lesson of the power of quilting to tell this story, and our roles in sustaining it.

Jan Wisor

RETREAT: IT WAS A GAS!

The first year I planned the retreat for our fledgling quilt group, I did all the planning and meal prep since they were so unsure about this whole going-away-to-quilt thing. I planned easy dinners that the attendees would help prepare, but for Friday night I had made our family's favorite chili recipe, which includes red kidney and black beans (and a touch of cocoa powder). At the time I didn't know that midwesterners were so unadventurous in their food choices (I'd moved to Fort Wayne from New York just a few years before). Most had never even heard of black beans, but everyone seemed to enjoy it along with the homemade cornbread.

As we continued to quilt after dinner, some of the women started to voice their concern about being a bit gassy. One woman had a serious issue, and every time the gas built up too much, she would run out into an enclosed stairwell. All would be quiet for a moment, and then we would hear her laugh hysterically, which of course made all of us laugh! She would then return to her sewing machine and continue to sew. This went on for a few hours, and by that time we were all laughing so hard, I am sure it hampered our sewing abilities! The next morning, those who had gone to bed earlier were curious about the evening's laughter. The hallway our gassy quilter ran to was the one leading to the bedrooms, and her laughter had echoed all the way up to the second floor!

The following year, I was not allowed to plan the menu for the weekend. (The group was taking ownership of the event! Yay!) The highlight of the weekend was the centerpieces for the dining tables—giant cans of beans decorated with fake flowers, supplied by an anonymous attendee!

Jackie Daugherty

WHAT'S FOR DINNER?

For 10 years, I had been asking my Facebook friends what they were having for dinner. I always loved the contributions of "a pint of ice cream" or "a handful of Lucky Charms." As the years went by, people would share with me that they used the posts as meal plans! Friends offered up recipes or sent links back and forth. There were simple and elaborate meals, and even funny posts requesting "reservations."

My friend Leslie Tucker Jenison and I both enjoy cooking and even had a blog, *Artists Cooking with Gas*, with tried-and-true recipes. In 2012, Carmen Beck from exhibits at Quilts, Inc., contacted me to propose a special exhibit for 2013 with the theme "What's for Dinner?" What a great idea!

So, what would dinner look like? Leslie and I thought that this needed to be shown as if the artists were gathering for a dinner party (inspired by Judy Chicago's amazing installation *The Dinner Party*), and the table was set. The quilt size would be a 24" × 15" horizontal format. We didn't want the exhibit to be hung in the typical manner of quilts at a show.

Because the place settings could be three-dimensional, we had some very unusual things on the plate (and off!). The artist's name was on a placard in front of their place setting, and we put each artist statement with details about the piece in a laminated "menu" stationed at each end of the installation.

The *What's for Dinner* exhibit premiered at the International Quilt Market and Festival 2013 in Houston. These enlarged "place settings," complete with a place mat / tablecloth, napkin, fork, knife, spoon, and a plateful of what the artist was eating for dinner, offered a variety of interpretations and views into different cultures, rituals, and lifestyles.

We set the tables with our dinner quilts in Houston, Chicago, and Long Beach. Quilters and food have always gone together, and this exhibit addressed that phenomenon through a variety of themes for 10 years. It was a great ride. Friends are still sharing their place settings on social media, even though I have stopped asking what they are having for dinner.

Jamie Fingal with Leslie Tucker Jenison

Food 163

CHAPTER 11

Celebration

Quilting is not just a hobby; it's an art form that weaves memories, emotions, and stories into every stitch. For many of us, quilting started when we anticipated the arrival of a new baby or a special occasion such as a niece's or nephew's birth. For my mother, quilts were made only for weddings, while I find joy in creating them for all occasions (especially red and green quilts, and double wedding rings . . .).

My passion for quilting was put to the test when my best friend's three daughters got married in three consecutive years. Each of them deserved a unique double-wedding-ring quilt that captured the essence of their love story. And with every quilt I made, I poured my heart and soul into it, weaving their love into the very fabric of the quilt.

Whenever I'm invited to a birthday party, I dive into my stash of finished quilts to find the perfect one to give. Because, let's face it, having a stash of finished quilts at the ready is something quilters are good at!

Over the years, there have been countless ways in which I've made quilts to celebrate. Have you ever organized signature blocks for a special event? The feeling of reading heartfelt messages from loved ones and incorporating them into a quilt is a celebration in itself.

Have you ever had your quilt hung in a quilt show? Been surprised by winning an award for your quilt? There's nothing quite like the feeling of recognition and appreciation for the art we love.

In the world of quilting, celebrations and quilting collide in beautiful and unexpected ways. Each quilt is a celebration of life, love, and the memories we hold dear.

But celebrating isn't always about making a quilt; sometimes it's about receiving one. I've read amazing stories of inmates in Missouri making quilts for foster children, Quilts of Valor thanking veterans for their service, Project Linus collecting for children. Anytime we can give a quilt, it's a celebration of love. Made by hand to give a quilted hug.

Quilting is a passion of mine, a way to bring beauty and comfort to the world around me. But it wasn't until my daughter was 10 years old that I truly realized the power of this craft to make a difference in the lives of others.

It started with a simple idea—to donate some of my quilts to a local shelter. But after hitting road-blocks with storage and logistics, I was left wondering where else I could make an impact.

Then, fate intervened. As I stood outside my daughter's school, chatting with another parent, I found myself explaining my love for quilting and my desire to help those in need. I had a vague idea that he worked for a transitional-housing organization but wasn't sure he'd know what to do with a quilt . . . to my surprise, he uttered the words that changed everything: "Do you have 700?"

I was stunned, but also inspired. And so, I set to work. I reached out to my blogging quilt community, asking for help in creating House blocks that could be turned into quilts for families transitioning out of homelessness. And the response was overwhelming—over 550 blocks poured in, and I spent countless hours piecing them together into 60 beautiful quilts. We ended up auctioning off those quilts and raised over $30,000 for the Acacia Network.

But I wasn't done yet. With each passing week, I then asked only for finished quilts, and soon they arrived in the mail! Quilters from all over the country joined in the effort. And as the pile grew to over 700, I knew it was time to make my way to the South Bronx, where I could see the impact of this project firsthand.

We made each event a "distribution celebration" for each of the buildings. As I handed out each quilt, watching as families wrapped themselves in warmth and comfort, I felt a sense of joy that's hard to describe. And with each hug I received, the name of the donor was read aloud; I knew that this was truly a community effort.

Quilting had always been a way for me to express myself, to create something beautiful out of scraps of fabric. But in that moment, I realized that it was so much more. It was a way to bring people together, to lift each other up, to make a tangible difference in the world, to celebrate. And I knew, without a doubt, that I would keep quilting—keep creating—for as long as I lived.

CELEBRATION: Jubilate Block

FOR THE 12" BLOCK:

Frame *solid light blue*

2 frames, frame template

2 triangles, small triangle template

Frame *solid purple*

2 reverse frames, reverse-frame template

2 triangles, small triangle template

Center Triangles *solid medium blue, red print*

2 triangles from each fabric, center triangle template

Swag *solid red*

2 swags, swag template

2 reverse swags, reverse swag template

Background *white print*

2 backgrounds, background template

2 reverse backgrounds, reverse background template

ASSEMBLY

1. Arrange block pieces as shown.

2. Align and sew a navy-blue frame triangle on a light-blue frame with right sides together. Press toward the navy-blue triangle. Make 2 units.

3. In the same manner, make two reverse-frame units with the opposite colors.

4. Sew a center triangle to each frame unit with right sides together, aligning the edges. Press seams toward the blue center triangles and away from the red triangles.

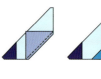

5. Transfer alignment mark from templates onto a swag and a background piece. Place the pieces right sides together, pinning at the marking and aligning the raw edges. The pieces fit together at both ends; pin to hold in place. Sew this curved seam with the **background piece on top**—"floppy toppy"! For curved-seam success, go slowly, keeping the raw edges of both curves together as you sew. Hold pieces at the middle pin, keeping the swag piece flat. The fabric bias of the background piece

will then set into that shape evenly as you align the raw edges. Gently press seam allowance toward the background. Make two of these units. In the same manner, make two reverse-swag units.

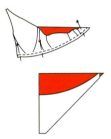

6. Sew the light-blue frame unit and swag unit together with right sides facing. Press toward the frame unit. Make 2 of these quarter squares.

7. In the same manner, make two reverse quarter squares, using the navy-blue frame units and reverse-swag units.

8. Sew a quarter-square unit to a reverse quarter-square unit with right sides together, pinning to match intersecting seams. Press seam open. Make two of these half-square units.

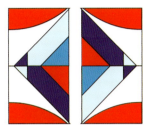

9. Pin and sew the two half-square units together to create a Jubilate block. Press seam open. Block measures 12½" × 12½".

BLOCKS NEEDED FOR EXPERIENCE QUILT

12" Jubilate blocks *make 2 blocks*

Celebration

169

Threads of Celebration

YOU WON!

I remember the day vividly when I decided to make my momma's dream come true by crafting her a stunning Dresden Plate quilt for Mother's Day. Though I had never attempted such a quilt before, I was determined to create something that would make her heart sing. And boy, did it ever!

But that wasn't the end of the story. My younger brother, who knew I had a knack for quilting, kept urging me to enter Momma's quilt into a quilt show. Now, I'm not one for the spotlight, but something about his persistent encouragement made me reconsider.

So, I mustered up the courage to call my momma and tell her the news. I had some good news and bad news. The good news was that I was going to enter her prized Dresden Plate quilt into the Smokey Mountain Quilt Show. The bad news was that she would have to wait to receive it.

My dear momma was thrilled beyond belief at the prospect of her quilt being showcased at such a prestigious event. As for me, I had no idea what to expect. The show was only a week away, and I hadn't received any news, so I assumed I hadn't won. That was until a phone call from a lovely lady from the guild came through one Friday afternoon.

She introduced herself and then, without much ado, announced that my momma's Dresden Quilt had won first prize! I couldn't contain my excitement and burst out screaming and jumping like a mad person, with the exhilaration of a *Price Is Right* winner on steroids. I swear I did more laps around my house than I could count!

I then called my momma to deliver the fantastic news, and she was equally overjoyed. We ended up going to the quilt show, and let me tell you, that was a barrel of laughs!

Penny Powell

THE GREAT LAKES GIFT

I was appraising quilts on the Space Coast of Florida several years back. A well-dressed elderly gentleman approached my table, gently carrying a quilt. As we put the quilt on the table, he handled it tenderly. "This quilt is special to you, isn't it?" I inquired.

"Oh, yes. My dear mother made this when I was a child."

The quilt was made of dark wools appliquéd with charming folk art motifs, birds, florals, various objects. As I worked, he chatted with onlookers who were admiring the quilt. He was delighted with the attention his beloved quilt was receiving. I interrupted a conversation to ask a question.

"Sir, was a member of your family in the Navy?"

"No, no, I don't believe so. Why do you ask?"

I showed the owner a buttonhole that had been sewn shut, a tiny trail of microscopic holes where a seam in the shape of a pocket had been removed, and other signs of a former life.

"I think these were uniforms," I said.

His hands flew to his cheeks, and tears filled his eyes. "My father was a merchant seaman on the Great Lakes! These would have been his uniforms! I thought this quilt was a gift from my mother, and now I see that my father gave as well."

After that, his were not the only teary eyes in the room!

Teddy Pruett

REUNITED

The final quilt crafted by my grandmother was intended to be raffled off for a church fundraiser. We had no way of knowing that it would be her last work of art. She passed away a few days after undergoing open-heart surgery, from an unrelated medical condition. My mother held on to the quilt while tickets were being sold in anticipation of the raffle.

Following my grandmother's funeral, my mother went to show the quilt to visitors, only to find it missing. We speculated that it may have been accidentally donated along with other items in black bags. Another quilt was donated in its place, but the loss only added to the already overwhelming grief we were experiencing.

Years later, when I moved into a new home, I stumbled upon the quilt in a closet. As it turned out, my husband had recognized the emotional value of the quilt at the time and knew it was meant to remain within our family rather than being raffled off. He had gone to my mother's house, taken the quilt, and entrusted it to a loyal family friend. This friend was sworn to secrecy and instructed not to open the bag. As my husband and I moved into our newly built house, he retrieved it and placed it in an upstairs closet for me to find.

In the end, we were overjoyed to have recovered this treasured piece of our family's history, and it serves as a celebration of my grandmother's talent and her unwavering love for her family.

Cindy Pilkington

CELEBRATION OF QUILTS

During my daughter's wedding reception in October 2018, my mother tearfully commented to me that it was the first time in years that all her children, along with our spouses and father, were in the same place. (We are spread out, living in Maine, Maryland, and Texas.) Her words saddened me, and my husband and I decided to surprise my parents the following year with a family vacation in Nags Head, North Carolina, during Christmas week. All three siblings, along with spouses and grandchildren, made arrangements to be there.

In January 2019, I embarked on a crazy project: making lap quilts as Christmas gifts for everyone. I managed to construct, quilt, and finish 13 quilts in just 11 months, without anyone knowing except my husband.

I purchased large holiday-themed gift bags and wrapped all the quilts for the eight-hour drive to the beach house. On Christmas Eve, we played the classic swap game, and as each person opened their gift bag, there were "oohs" and "ahhs." The surprise came when the second person opened their bag and realized that everyone would be receiving a quilt. I had made both feminine- and masculine-themed quilts to suit everyone's taste.

There was laughter and trading as family members "stole" from each other, but eventually, everyone went to bed with a cozy quilt made with love. It was a week that I will never forget.

Patty Hammond

Q: Tell me if you've ever used quilt making to get through a difficult time.

In the early 1990s, my father was diagnosed with lung cancer, and I was in my studio, pretty much all of the time, and I was very, very busy making quilts because I couldn't deal with the ramifications of losing him. So, I made a lot of quilts at that time, and they were all out of the same fabric, this wonderful, not-quite-Christmas red, but maybe a cherry red, and then a green and a cream. I kind of did a Christmas-themed collection; I was working and working and working. I have runners and I have quilts and I have pillows. It just got me through some of that pain and let me try to make some happiness happen. That was a really difficult time and I think that focusing on making this kind of suite of Christmas decoration type quilts helped me get through it. [. . .]

Q: *What have you done with those quilts?*

I have them and I bring them out at Christmas. Shortly before he was diagnosed with lung cancer, my parents celebrated their 50th wedding anniversary. My dad bought my mom a new Bernina sewing machine. And she being a Singer girl didn't like it, so then he decided he was going to learn how to quilt. My father was also making quilts during his illness, and he made a special quilt for me. He was very fond of Eleanor Burns because he enjoyed reading her books and her geometric ways of cutting made sense to his carpenter mind. He would cut his own templates and have fun. He made me a queen-size triple Irish chain out of the same fabric that I was using to get through his deteriorating health. When I bring these things out, it's like a great remembrance of him and how much inspiration he was for me. [. . .]

Q: *What did your dad think of your quiltmaking?*

I think he was very proud it. My interest in quilting was the impetus for his trying quilting. And I just think it was funny; here was this seventy-something-year-old man cranking out these quilts. My mother said that she would never quilt because of course her mother quilted and she didn't like it. But then I sort [of] got her hooked on it. She and I took a couple of classes together and a couple of my aunts on my father's side took these classes with us. It was really fun. Then I think he saw how fun it was and he didn't want this Bernina to sit and go to waste so he decided, "I think I'm going start doing quilting." He was having fun. And I think he was proud that all of us were quilting. He was always the sewing-machine fix-it man. If anything went wrong, he could always get them up and running again. He just liked to tinker with things, and he wasn't afraid to create. I think my mom was a little jealous when he was quilting because it came easy for him. And she got stuck doing the bindings and such because he wasn't going to sit and do that. He just wanted to get the tops done. [*Laughs.*]

Kimberlee Madsen
interviewed by Karen Musgrave for the Quilt Alliance's Quilters' Save Our Stories (QSOS) project, August 28, 2008
www.qsos.quiltalliance.org/items/show/2615

WRAPPED IN COMFORT AND WONDER

My earliest recollections consist of burrowing under quilts crafted by the hands of my great-grandma Gertie. During naptime, I'd stay wide eyed, inspecting the lovingly hand-sewn remnants of clothing and drapes pieced together into quilts for family members. I distinctly remember nibbling on white dots affixed to navy-blue fabric, and to this day, I'm still curious about the origins of the red-and-gray fabric with atomic designs—perhaps a pair of men's pajamas, a shirt, or a dress?

Quilting and sewing runs deep in the women of my family, and my mother and I proudly continue the legacy of quilts that date back to my great-grandmothers. On my father's side, our family hails from South Dakota, where they sewed utilitarian quilts by using scraps of fabric, solids, and feed sack fabrics. My dad recollects playing under the big quilting frame during quilting bees at Gertie's house, alongside her sister Delia and their daughters. It was a day filled with laughter and cherished memories.

Meanwhile, my mother's side of the family deliberately purchased fabric for their quilts. Great-Grandma Matilda Frederika Cook Sinclair was a master embroiderer, quilter, and baker extraordinaire. Grandma Til, as my mom remembers her, specialized in popular quilt patterns such as solid yellow and Triple Irish Chain, Parasol Garden Ladies, and a beautiful apple blossom appliqué quilt that we believe is credited to Fairfield kits.

When I was growing up, my mother sewed all of our clothes, and it was only natural that I learn as well. I started out at an early age with cardboard lace-up cards before graduating to crafting doll clothes on a tiny pink sewing machine. My first foray into garment making resulted in two wrap miniskirts with huge yellow smiley faces on a white backdrop. Paired with yellow leotard tops and white granny boots, my sister and I were quite the sight during our visit to Disneyland in the early 1970s.

I embarked on quilting at age 14 but swiftly decided that cutting out tiny pieces and piecing them back together was far too arduous. Little did I know that the future held the promise of rotary cutters and die-cutting machines.

When my son Matt was a baby, I repurposed the batting from my favorite comforter into a quilt. The print featured blue, green, red, and yellow dinosaurs, and this quilt remained his favorite long after dinosaurs lost their charm. It had the ability to comfort him when he wasn't feeling well, and to keep him cozy at night. In the years that followed, I gifted many quilts to Matt and his wife, Annie. Seeing them draped over their sofa and knowing that the legacy of providing comfort continues fills me with joy.

Last night, we learned that we are soon to become grandparents. My heart overflows with happiness, and my mind is already designing the baby quilt. It's time to revel in life's blessings.

Chris Daly

QUILTING PARTY

We have a lot of quilters in our family—but that wasn't always the case. Though a few of us were already quilting, I'd say it really started when my sister-in-law Jessica made plans to go to Quiltfest, an annual summer week of workshops, events, and fabric shopping sponsored by Tennessee Quilts, a local quilt shop my mom loves. Not to be left out, I decided to fly down to Tennessee too. This five-day event was so much fun—we each went to different classes during the day, then fabric-shopped for goodies together, then went home to my parents' lake house for dinner and a swim, before staying up late into the night, laughing, catching up on each other's lives, sharing tidbits with each other from our famous quilter-teachers as if we were their lifelong BFFs.... Mary Lou says it's better if you do it *this* way, Karen likes the way *I* use color in my quilts...that kind of silly banter kept us going as we sewed like crazy from the day's class.

Quiltfest also boasted a large catered banquet with a lecture from one of the teachers and show-and-tell from attendees. We weren't so sure about that event—it might cut into valuable sewing time—but my mom convinced us to give it a shot. It was fun to see people's projects and be inspired by the quilting lecture and eat yummy southern food. We were impressed by—and jealous of!—two larger groups of friends who attended together every year.

What memories and stories the three of us had from those few days! When your hobby isn't one that most of your friends know anything about, it's great fun to be surrounded by a bunch of other enthusiasts. It's also easy to laugh at ourselves and what may seem to outsiders "our strange ways." We still giggle over the exhortation from one show-and-tell participant, as she insistently told the audience, "When you see sea turtle fabric, buy it!" after showing her quilt and telling about the search for the fabrics she wanted to use.

Well, when other members of our family heard Jessica and I talk about Quiltfest, they wanted in, even if they didn't quilt. So we started by inviting my Gran, aunt, and cousin for the next year, then an aunt and cousins on another side of the family. Some of them came just to be a part of the fun, not taking classes, no intentions of quilting, just enjoying the time together. My cousin, Erin, came to scrapbook while we quilted... and left with a queen-size quilt she made from start to finish. When she completed the quilting, we cranked up the music and she took a victory lap around the room, quilt flying behind her! We would take turns preparing meals, making more time for sewing, relaxing, fabric shopping, and spending time with these four generations we didn't get to see often enough.

For several years we all would converge on eastern Tennessee for Quiltfest, to celebrate quilts and quilting. We had a baby shower one year, and also birthday parties, and even celebrated a particularly abundant zucchini year by each contributing a different zucchini dish at every meal. We became one of the big groups at the banquet—three generations of women showing off our quilting-themed temporary tattoos! We even did some round robin and block swap collaborative quilts to keep us more connected throughout the rest of the year. Some of us are still "once-a-year" quilters, and though the Quiltfest event is no more, we still feel the pull to gather and connect for a few days of quilting—and it's *always* a party!

Kim Hryniewicz

Celebration

CHAPTER 12

New Adventures

My fondness for sewing intuitively, without the constraints of patterns, led me to discover my tribe among the Quilt Mavericks and Rebel Quilters (improv groups). It was a joyous moment to find like-minded individuals who shared my passion for free-form quilting. While my quilt designs now incorporate traditional block styles built in improvisational ways, my muse leads me on a daily flip-flopping journey of inspiration, always seeking out new and unconventional ways to approach my art.

I am an improv quilter at heart, constantly experimenting and pushing boundaries. My design process involves creating on my design wall, cutting more fabric than I could possibly use in one quilt, and stashing away the leftovers for future scrap quilts or even art quilts. The beauty I find in my process lies in the limitless possibilities and the absence of constraints in my thinking.

As I journey further down the path of quilting, my fascination with block patterns continues to deepen. I find myself drawn to the timeless beauty of old quilts, listening intently to the voices of quilters past as I study their works. Each piece is a treasure trove of inspiration, with color choices and stitches that resonate with me on a personal level.

I look forward to the way my process and styles of work change. I seem to ebb and flow among a variety of styles, enjoying each new exploration as I go. Sometimes I need a big difficult project to work on, and sometimes just a simple block repeat suffices. Sometimes a limited palette of color is all I need, and others I want hundreds of colors washed across my cutting table. Perhaps a little surface design creeps in; other times it's embroidery . . . wherever I wander, it's always a happy place to be.

The next part of my journey is one I eagerly await to present itself to me. I never know when I will be inspired, but following that spark as my guiding force is still the thing that excites me most. I encourage change, since I know it shifts the way I see, think, and feel, which are all ways for me to dig deeper in what I express in my stitches. It's a magical experience, one that allows me to tap into my innermost thoughts, skills, and techniques and bring them to life through the beauty of quilting.

The challenges and changes that life throws at us, interrupting our daily plans, are always opportunities that we can then create from. Perhaps it even helps the transition of change, since it allows us to express ourselves in ways we might not otherwise do.

I also think about what adventures my quilts will have—how they affect the people who receive them, how they will be here long after I am gone. I wonder which ones will last the longest, which ones my daughter will cherish, and if people years after I'm gone will wonder, "What was she thinking when she made that?". . . it is precious to ponder.

What has quilting added to your life? Has it given you a voice?

I continue to look for my people. Quilt guilds and groups have been an essential part of community. If you haven't found a guild, keep trying. Stand up and share at show-and-tell, and the ones who like what you do come to you. Be proud of your work and label your quilts so that years from now, people can say your name and see themselves in your stitches. The thread bond continues to connect each and every one of us.

I wonder what next great random quilt connection will happen that will bring me a new adventure. Whatever it is, I plan to capture those special moments in my work. Quilts are a diary of our lives, and of course a great quilted hug! What a gift!

NEW ADVENTURES: Bunting Block

FOR THE 12" BLOCK:

Small Triangles *assorted prints*

1 square 4¼" × 4¼" each from assorted prints; cut each square in half diagonally in both directions (4 triangles from each square); 16 small triangles needed.

Background *white print*

4 squares 4¼" × 4¼"; cut each square in half diagonally in both directions (4 triangles from each square); 16 small triangles needed.

8 squares 3⅞" × 3⅞"; cut each square in half diagonally in one direction (2 triangles from each square); 16 large triangles needed.

ASSEMBLY

1. Lay out a bright small triangle, a white small triangle, and a white large triangle as shown. With right sides together, sew the two small triangles together, pressing away from the white small triangle.

2. Sew the white large triangle to the long side of the pieced triangle unit. Press toward the pieced unit. Trim dog-ears to complete a bunting unit*. Make 16 bunting units, using various prints.

3. Lay out 16 bunting units as shown. Sew units into rows. Sew the rows together. Press seams open or to one side. Block measures 12½" × 12½".

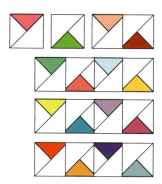

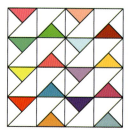

182

Chapter 12

BLOCKS NEEDED FOR EXPERIENCE QUILT

12" Bunting blocks *make 2 blocks*

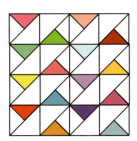 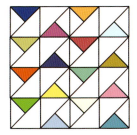

EXTRA BITS NEEDED FOR EXPERIENCE QUILT

Bunting units *make 24 units*

*This unit is also used to make the final borders. See p. 191.

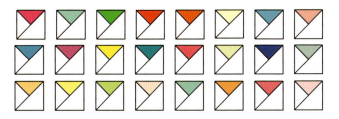

New Adventures

Threads of New Adventures

Q: *How do you want to be remembered?*

As a wild and crazy quilt lady [*laughs*] who wasn't afraid to use color and pattern. I think that would probably be the best way to put it. And I think, hopefully that someone would say, "She had an eye for design." Maybe not always doing it herself all the time but recognizing it in other things. And that I was an interesting person. An interesting quilter. Quirky maybe but that's okay.

Kimberlee Madsen
interviewed by Karen Musgrave for the Quilt Alliance's Quilters' Save Our Stories (QSOS) project, August 28, 2008
www.qsos.quiltalliance.org/items/show/2615

WHAT'S A GUILD?

Between a cross-country move, the pandemic, and working from home, I forgot how to socialize. It wasn't that I disliked people. It's just that meeting new ones filled me with an incredible amount of anxiety. How does one navigate small talk? Do I even own real pants anymore?

I'd been ducking out of view of delivery drivers and door-to-door pest control salespeople for over a year when I met my neighbor. She made it through my defenses only because she caught me walking my dog. The road in front of my house is a popular thoroughfare for the health conscious. I learned to time my quick jaunts into the yard with off-peak walking times. On the day I crossed paths with the woman down the street, I'd made a miscalculation in my timing.

As fate would have it, she was much more outgoing than me. She struck up a conversation. My instinct was to panic, but within a few moments I realized that this was a kind person trying to make a connection. After a brief chat, she popped the question that would take us from two neighborhood walkers to people on a real outing together.

"Do you want to come to a guild meeting with me on Friday?"

I agreed to go. I didn't give myself time to overthink it. She seemed so nice, and I had to admit that underneath the thick carapace of self-reliance and social anxiety, I longed for friendship and camaraderie. After an exchange of phone numbers, she was on her way.

Back inside, I had to look up what a guild was. Before this, I thought they were for medieval silversmiths. A quick search and some recollection of her interest in sewing helped me reach the right conclusion. It turns out that guilds are full of quilters.

184   Chapter 12

Then I had to figure out what happens at guild meetings. Most people would have asked the person who invited them. I opted to neurotically search the internet instead. I threw a few items from my meager sewing supplies into a Ziploc bag just in case we were expected to sew on the spot. At the time, I was interested in different textile traditions, but I definitely wasn't a quilter.

This didn't seem to be a problem for the folks in the guild, though. They showered me with scraps and tools they no longer needed. I thought I might make one friend by agreeing to go to this mysterious meeting, but now I'm blessed with many.

My world is bigger and better because of quilts and their makers. I'm so glad I said yes.

Angelina Holt

CAREER CHANGE

I became a professional longarm quilter and changed my life completely without even fully realizing how unhappy I had been in my career. For over 30 years, I had worked a full-time office job. Making quilts brought me such great joy that I always found a little time to stitch, even it was a quick 20 minutes before I went to work. When my pile of quilts kept growing, I decided on a whim to purchase a longarm machine sight unseen and teach myself to quilt so that I could finish my many quilt tops. I justified this very expensive purchase to my husband by telling him I might be able to take some quilts in from customers to help pay for it. He was very open minded and supportive and told me to go for it.

When the longarm was delivered and set up, I was taught how to turn it on, how to thread the machine, and all the technical skills to run it. To say I was excited is an understatement. I played on my new machine every evening after work and on weekends, just practicing designs and finishing my tops. Some of the first ones are pretty bad, but they show the journey, and I still have them to remind myself how far I have come. When you want something so badly, you find a way to make it happen. This began my journey to teach myself to learn how to longarm quilt without the aid of taking classes. It opened up my world and I realized this was a whole different way to add design and dimension to my quilts.

About six months into my crazy adventure, my sister-in-law said I had to visit a local quilt shop near her in Walla Walla, Washington, called Stash. I brought several quilts I had worked on and met with the owners: Kristen, Kathy, and Ann. They loved what I was doing and took my card. Next thing I knew, I had a box of 10 quilt tops with a note inside saying, "Do whatever you like, practice, and have fun." Stash hung all the quilts I had worked on, and my business was growing. I formed the best friendships with those ladies, and I talk to Kristen almost daily as we have become very good friends.

New Adventures

Three years later, I was able to quit my full-time job and take the leap of faith to do just longarm quilting. It was the scariest thing I've ever done. Now I have two machines and lot of wonderful customers that keep coming back. Never in my wildest dreams did I think I'd quit a good-paying, stable job to doodle on people's quilts. This longarm business was definitely never the plan, but I sure am glad it happened. As they always say, "Love what you do, and you will never work a day in your life." I plan to do that for the rest of mine!

Teresa Silva

ONE GIRL, TWO STAGES

If you recognize my name, it's probably because you're familiar with work I've done in the quilt world over the past 12 years. It's likely *not* because you know me from my work as a professional writer and performance artist. But from the ages of 26 to 31, that's how I earned a living.

As a writer, I freelanced for various publishing companies (*The Amazing Book of Dogs!*, *Understanding Your HVAC*—that sort of thing). But my main gig was as a member of the Neofuturists, one of the most highly regarded experimental theater companies in the country, founded in Chicago in 1988. The Neos are world famous for a show called *Too Much Light Makes the Baby Go Blind*. The show is described as "an ever-changing attempt to perform 30 plays in 60 minutes."

It works like this: Ensemble members write short plays throughout the week and pitch them on Tuesday night. Plays are selected and rehearsed. Then you go home. You spend the next three days learning your lines and choreography. You make your own props. When Friday night rolls around, you show up at the theater and get a couple more hours to rehearse together while a long line of eager audience members forms around the block. The doors open at 11:30 p.m., and each audience member gets a menu that lists the titles of all 30 plays in the show that night. A darkroom timer is set for 60 minutes, and then the show begins. Oh, and the audience determines the order in which the plays are performed each night. Once a play ends, the audience is instructed to shout out the number of the next play they want to see. It's absolute pandemonium. Three shows a weekend. And it really is a race every time to get all 30 plays performed within one hour. Sometimes we'd make it; sometimes we wouldn't.

The six years I spent as a Neo remain six of the most creatively rewarding years of my life. Anyone who's ever seen *Too Much Light* knows the power of the show. It is by turns hilarious, heartbreaking, thought provoking, and weird, and above all, it is wonderful. The raw talent in the cast, the breathless pace of the work, the athleticism required, the fun of it all—I don't suppose I'll ever be able to properly express my gratitude for all that.

So there I am, actually paying the rent as a writer-performer in the big city. And then my mom, Marianne Fons, and her business partner Liz Porter sell their company. The corporation that bought it suddenly had a problem: What do you do with a brand called Fons & Porter when Fons and Porter retire?

About a year before that, I had started making quilts. I was 28. When the Powers That Be at Fons & Porter got wind of this, it was a lucky break: they could foster a "Fons 2.0" and take the brand into the next generation. When they asked me if I wanted to guest-host on Mom's TV show, I said yes immediately. Look, I was making a living as a writer-performer, but I needed the gig.

I went on the show. And everything changed.

Mary Fons

Q: Tell me about the quilt you brought today. Who made it, where was it made, and how old is the particular pattern?

I am so thrilled to be able to talk about this particular quilt because it was my very first quilt. I was a young girl growing up in San Francisco and had never had any background in stitchery. My grandmother knitted, but I don't recall she ever sewed. This particular quilt was the outgrowth of a summer project. Alice Zwanck of St. John's Presbyterian Church invited the high school girls to join her one summer to learn how to sew. She called all of us and said, "Oh, I thought it would be nice if we could maybe have a quilting bee." I thought about this. I was sixteen years old, and said, "Oh, thank you for calling, but I don't think I am interested in sewing." So that ended our first conversation. Next week Alice called back and she said, "Well, I've kind of rethought what we will do for our summer. I've invited the boys to come and learn how to play bridge with my husband at 8:00 on Wednesday nights, and we can have the girls come at 7:00. We could have cookies and maybe do a little bit of sewing. How does that sound?" Well, she got ten of us there the very next week! [*Laughter.*] And for me that was my introduction to sewing. So, it's through her that I have to give a lot of credit for the excitement and the enthusiasm that I still continue to feel about quilting.

Q: And that summer, did you each have your own project, and this was the result of it, or did you work on one quilt together?

No, we each made choices. We looked at many, many books. This particular pattern, Dahlia, came from somebody's aunt who worked with the Dorcas Quilters of St. John's. I was just captivated with this pattern, because it was colorful, and had large pieces that I could handle. That summer I was working at Levi Strauss Company and I was in the department that did a lot of ordering for their sport shirts. So, I was always given the samples as they were discontinued. The pieces were the right size for the dahlia petals. This quilt really has a combination of Levi Strauss samples and anything I could beg, borrow, or snitch. [. . .]

Q: Tell me about how you made it. Is it an appliquéd top?

Yes. Alice and I were both learning how to quilt together, really. She kept one step ahead of me. Since this pattern came specifically from another person, I looked at it, and thought I could draw it out. Alice said, "Yes, we can draft that." So she and I drafted the pattern together. I didn't know you needed to do things in a block arrangement. I prepared the whole cloth background, which is the yellow and I appliquéd each one of those flowers to it. I was always lugging around this big hunk of yellow material [*laughter*], and carefully hand-stitching the flowers down. If you were to measure this quilt, it might be a little askew, but to my eye it looked alright. One night, Pat Zwank, who was Alice's husband, recognized that not too many girls were working on their quilt tops. Since everybody had chosen different patterns, each girl had a different outlook on the progress of her top. Some preferred to sew, others just wanted to eat cookies or play bridge with the guys. Pat decided on a little competition. He promised that the first girl to complete her quilt would be taken to dinner at Scomas Restaurant on the wharf. I accepted his challenge and two years later, Pat took Alice and I out to dinner.

New Adventures

[. . .] Then that year, 1958, Alice encouraged me to enter the Dahlia quilt in the California State Fair. I felt so special because here I was a city girl, and I was in the home-economics building. It was fun to see it hanging in the show. It didn't win any ribbons, but that didn't matter. Alice felt that she had accomplished a lot in two years by just encouraging me.

Bonita Morley
interviewed by Amy Henderson for the Quilt Alliance's Quilters' Save Our Stories (QSOS) project, May 31, 2001
www.qsos.quiltalliance.org/items/show/1501

Q: Was it difficult to give the quilt away?

No. I never have a problem giving a quilt away because when I make a quilt, I like the fact that I'm stitching it for someone else. But I do have a funny story about giving a quilt away. [. . .]

My son was about six, he is twenty-four now, and when I tell the story now he always goes "Oh mom." But I had made a quilt for this really good friend of ours that was getting married. This man was a confirmed bachelor, and he was finally getting married. I had made this kaleidoscope quilt and I dyed all the fabric for the border and my son helped me stir the dye, so he was a very important part of this quilt. I hand quilted the whole thing.

As we were on our way to FedEx to ship it, my son looked at me and said, "I want this quilt." And I was so shocked, and I said, "Well it is not your quilt. It's Steve's quilt and we are going to mail it to him in like two minutes." So, he didn't say anything else until we get to FedEx and he says again, "I want the quilt." And I say, "No honey you can't have the quilt." I FedExed the quilt overnight to Ojai, California.

That night my son said, "You know what I'm going to do? I'm going to pray that the quilt comes back." I said, "Well, you can't do that, Brian." And he said, "Absolutely that is what I'm going to do." I said, "No, no, that is not what you pray for." He said, "Nope, you said I could talk to God about whatever I wanted, I'm going to pray that the quilt comes back." I just said, "Fine, go ahead." And he says, "Fine, I will."

A couple days went by and I didn't hear from anyone in Ojai, and I was like, "Wow, I kind of wish I had a call saying they had gotten the quilt." I thought, "Oh, maybe they are busy with the wedding. Whatever." Then I get a call two days later from FedEx in Chicago and they say, "You have a package here." Now my mother used to send me packages all the time, so I never thought anything of it. I picked my son up from school and we went to FedEx, and there is the quilt package sitting there. I asked FedEx what happened. They said [. . .] "It went all the way there, and we must have gone to the wrong house or something. And because you had signature required and we couldn't find somebody by that name, we brought it back." My son who is standing in FedEx with me looks at me, and I went, "Fine, it is your quilt." [*Laughs.*] I made this couple another quilt and gave it to them for their first wedding anniversary. I still have that first quilt. I renamed it the "Boomerang Quilt" and I'm going to give it to Brian on his wedding.

Crane Johnson
interviewed by Karen Musgrave for the Quilt Alliance's Quilters' Save Our Stories (QSOS) project, August 4, 2008
www.qsos.quiltalliance.org/items/show/2597

MOVING ON UP!

After graduating from college in St. Paul, Minnesota, I moved to Duluth in 1993. My fiancé and I were lucky enough to live in an adorable pink house, which had once belonged to his grandmother. We were renovating the home while living there, which is always quite a challenge.

One of the obstacles we faced was privacy in the room facing the busy street. Without curtains, I decided to get creative and tack up the red, yellow, and blue calico half-square triangle quilt top I had hand-pieced. With great care and enthusiasm, I fashioned this beautiful piece into a makeshift window covering, which not only provided us with much-needed privacy but also added a touch of rustic elegance to the house's Craftsman style.

However, not everyone appreciated our creative solution. We soon learned that some members of the family, who lived in the area, had driven by and commented that our house "looked like a bunch of hippies lived there."

I'm going to assume it was purely because of the house color . . . and not the bohemian chic energy my lovely quilt top emanated.

Victoria Findlay Wolfe

New Adventures

The Experience Quilt Construction

I love puzzles—do you? Now the fun begins! This might look daunting, but trust me, it's not . . . I recommend reading all the way through the construction before you begin, and laying out your quilt following the quilt layout diagram on page 196.

THE EXPERIENCE QUILT: EXTRA BITS

Make the extra bits and borders at this point so you can add in the colors you want to see more in your quilt. I decided what colors to use by looking at the full picture of my blocks and what those little bits will be sitting next to.

Do you have a favorite color you want to highlight in these units?

Do you need to add a few darker/brighter/lighter or juicer colors to dance your eye around the quilt?

Or can they just be random and scrappy?

A bit of wisdom on making your blocks harmonious (working with your own color palette): If you feel that your blocks look even toned or muddy together, this is the time to *jazz up* a couple of units and make a few alternatives, and/or pick brighter and higher-contrasting colors for the extra bits to add a *value change*, which helps with the overall movement in the quilt. I chose mostly red/oranges and blues/greens for these scrappy units, since I tend to *see* those colors the most when I looked at the full layout of my quilt.

Instructions for Extra Bits:

Spirited Star, page 35

Constant Classic, page 47

Transit, page 129

Bunting, page 183

THE EXPERIENCE QUILT: BORDERS

When selecting your border color, a good trick is pulling a highly used color from the center of the quilt but in a slightly different value. Letting that color repeat at the outside of the quilt helps balance the entire visual. I chose a deeper red than the cherry-toned colors in the center of the quilt. Red is also a color I chose to continually sprinkle around the quilt design.

CUTTING:

Small Triangles *dark red*

24 squares 4¼" × 4¼"; cut each square in half diagonally in both directions (4 triangles from each square); 96 small triangles needed.

Background *white*

24 squares 4¼" × 4¼"; cut each square in half diagonally in both directions (4 triangles from each square); 96 small triangles needed.

48 squares 3⅞" × 3⅞"; cut each square in half diagonally in one direction (2 triangles from each square); 96 large triangles needed.

Make 96 Bunting units (p. 182). Sew the blocks together in strips of 24 Bunting units each, with the dark-red triangles pointing in the same direction. Press seams to one side. Borders each measure 3½" × 72½".

make 4

The Experience Quilt Construction

THE EXPERIENCE QUILT: ASSEMBLY

I've broken this quilt down into four sections for ease of construction. **Section 1** is the center strip of blocks. There are NO partial seams in this first section.

Sections 2–4 are constructed with as few partial seams as possible. If you think of each of these "sewn sections" afterward as a *block*, it makes the process clear, and success follows easily. Remember, a partial seam just means you start sewing a straight seam, and you stop 1"–2" before the end of the shortest piece . . . you come back later and finish the straight seam. EASY!

When you're sewing sections together, blocks often do not line up with one another; hence this kitchen sink style, which is not on a grid. Be sure to place a pin at the beginning and end of the seam/section, then add pins where needed to hold pieces together evenly. Refer to the section diagrams to see if any seams are meant to connect, and pin those points.

As you sew this first column of blocks together, you will be wondering about pressing the seam allowances. A couple of additions to the general Pressing Matters tips (pages 23–24):

- Most of the time I'm pressing to one side in this quilt. You will notice when you need to press a seam open to make it lay better, depending on your own blocks.

- For pressing partial seams, press only the beginning part that is sewn, to make it easy to add the next piece. Finish pressing the seam when you have completed sewing it.

The Experience Quilt layout is based on two sides (sections 2–4) and a center column (section 1). The "two sides" are exactly the same. After being constructed, the right side is rotated 180 degrees, to form the right side of the quilt. So, either make two of each section 2–4 as you go . . . or . . . focus on finishing those sections for the left side of quilt. Then go back and repeat the construction of sections 2–4 to make the pieces for the right side of the quilt—whatever you are most comfortable with.

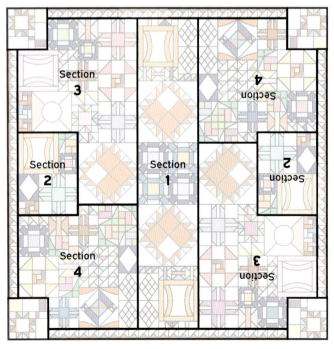

SECTION 1

1. Sew together (2) 9" Facets and (2) 9" Facets Variation blocks as shown to create center section 1.

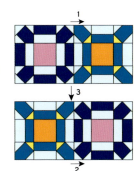

2. Section 1B: (1) Bear Paw Heart block, (1) Loops & Lines block, (3) 4" Bestie blocks, (2) Polished Diamond blocks, and Extra Bits from Spirited Star (p. 35): (3) half-square triangle units, and (1) block strip to create each section 1B.

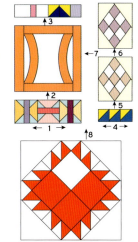

   Sew the blocks together, following the order indicated by the numbered arrows on the diagrams, pinning and pressing each addition.

3. Repeat step 2 to make the second 1B section.

4. Complete section 1 by sewing the bottom edge of the two 1B sections to the top and bottom of the center 1A section.

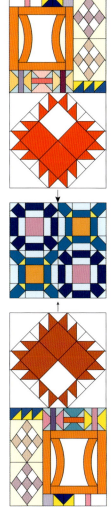

SECTION 2

1. Section 2 blocks: (1) 6" Facets block, (1) 6" Floris block, (1) Loops & Lines block, (1) Polished Diamond block, (1) 12" Transit block, (2) squares from Spirited Star (p. 35), and (1) center unit from Constant Classic (p. 47).

2. Sew the blocks together, following the order indicated by the diagram numbers, pinning and pressing each addition.

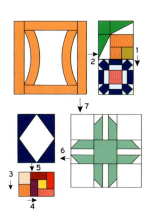
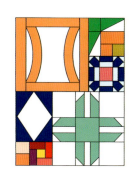

SECTION 3

1. Sew (2) 12" Transit blocks to (1) Constant Classic block as shown to create section 3A.

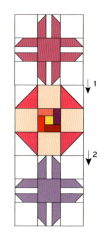

2. Section 3B blocks: (1) Dimensions block, (1) star from Spirited Star (p. 35), (2) Bunting units (p. 183), and Extra Bits from Constant Classic (p. 47): (3) center units and (2) half-square triangle units. Sew the blocks together, in the order indicated on the diagram, pinning and pressing each addition.

- The last seam is a partial seam. Sew the Bunting units on, stopping about 2" from the end and securing with a small backstitch.

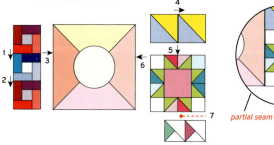

partial seam

The Experience Quilt Construction

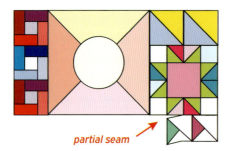

3. Section 3C blocks: (1) 9" Transit block, (1) Loops & Lines block, (1) 6" Bestie block, (1) 6" Facets block, (1) 9" Facets block, and (5) Bunting units (p. 183).

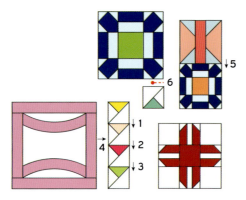

Sew the blocks together, in the order indicated on the diagram, pinning and pressing each addition.

- The last seam is a partial seam. Starting with the edges of those blocks aligned at the right side, sew about 1", then secure with a short backstitch.

4. Work your way around the Bunting unit, sewing on the blocks in the order shown. Align and pin the block edges at the start and end of each seam.

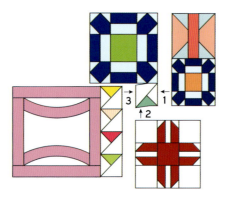

When you get to the third side, move the Facets block out of the way to get to the loose edge of the Bunting unit, and sew the seam, pinning the start and end.

5. At this point, you can close the initial partial seam farther... but not all the way! The edges of the blocks are still uneven here, waiting for the borders and corner block. Fold the right sides together at the partial seam and sew to about 2" from the end of the Facets block.

- This is a place in the quilt where there isn't anything to line up the end of the block (Facets). It is still important to pin the block wherever it lies, BEFORE sewing, so you don't stretch one side or the other.

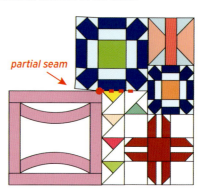

6. Sew sections 3B and 3C together. Then sew section 3A to the side. Last, add (1) 18" Bear Paw Heart block to complete section 3.

- There will be two partial seams still loose at this point.

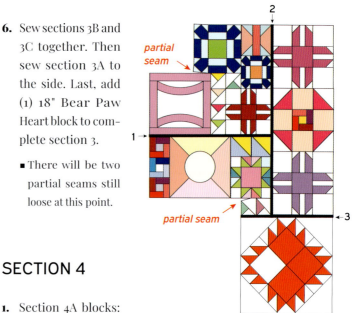

SECTION 4

1. Section 4A blocks: (3) Bunting units (p. 183), (1) 9" Facets block, (1) 6" Bestie block, and (1) 6" Floris block. Sew the blocks together, in the order indicated on the diagram, pinning and pressing each addition.

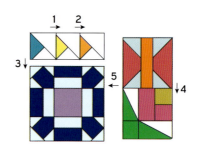

194

Chapter 12

2. Section 4B blocks: (1) Constant Classic block, (1) 6" Bestie block, (1) 6" Floris block, and (1) 9" Transit block. Sew the blocks together, in the order indicated on the diagram, pinning and pressing each addition.

    - The last seam is a partial seam. Stop sewing about 2" before the end of the Transit block, then secure with a short backstitch.

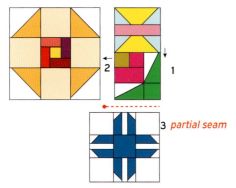

3. Section 4C blocks: (1) Bunting block, (1) Jubilate block, and (3) Polished Diamond blocks. Sew the blocks together, in the order indicated on the diagram, pinning and pressing each addition.

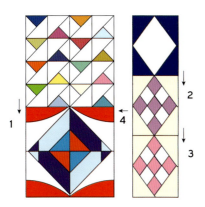

4. Section 4D blocks: (1) 12" Floris block, (1) 9" Transit block, (2) Bunting units (p. 183), and (1) 3½" square from Transit block (p. 129). Sew the blocks together, in the order indicated on the diagram, pinning and pressing each addition.

    - Seams #2 and #4 are partial seams. Stop sewing about 1"–2" before the end of the shorter side, then secure with a short backstitch.

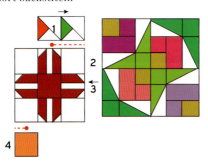

5. Work your way around the 3½" square (sewn last onto section 4D), sewing on the block sections in the order shown. Align and pin the block edges at the start and end of each seam. When you get to the third side, move the rest of section 4D out of the way to get to the loose edge of the square, and sew the seam, pinning the start and end.

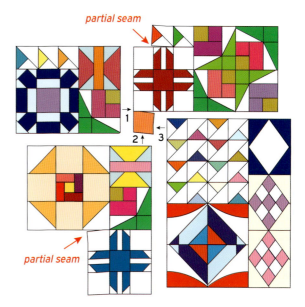

6. At this point, you can close the partial seam to complete section 4.

    - There will be two partial seams still loose at this point.

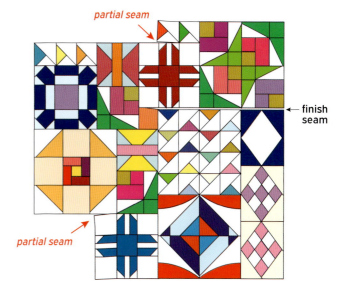

The Experience Quilt Construction 195

SEWING SECTIONS TOGETHER

1. Sew sections 3 and 4 together at the Bear Paw Heart block, as shown.

2. Next, sew section 2 to the Bear Paw Heart block / Bunting units, moving sections 3 and 4 out of the way to access the ends of this seam.

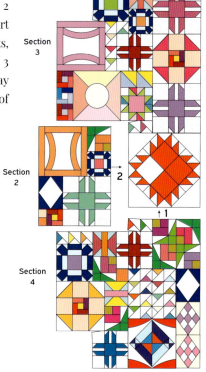

3. At the top and bottom of section 2, complete the partial seams all the way to the edge of the quilt.

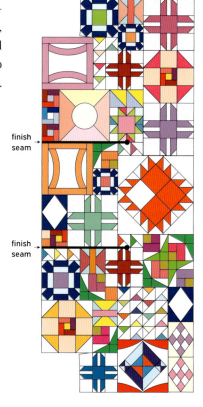

4. Sew this set of sections 2/3/4 to the left side of section 1.

5. Make a second set of sections 2, 3, and 4, sewing them together in the same order.

6. Rotate this 2/3/4 section 180 degrees and sew it to the right side of section 1.

7. Attach a border unit to each side of the quilt top center.

8. Sew the top left corner Spirited Star block to the side of the Facets block/border, paying attention to the orientation of the star. Then fold the block down so

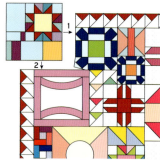

196   Experience Quilt Construction

you can then complete the Loops & Lines / border partial seam to the outside edge of the quilt.

9. In the same way, sew in the bottom right Spirited Star block. Sew the remaining two Spirited Star blocks to the side of the Transit block/border, then to the Constant Classic block/border to complete the quilt top.

FINISHING

1. Cut the 8½ yards of backing fabric into (3) 102" × WOF (width of fabric) panels.

    Trim the selvages from the fabric lengths. Using a ½" seam allowance, sew the panels together and trim to make a backing that measures approximately 102" × 102". Press the seams to one side.

2. Layer the quilt top, batting, and backing.

3. Quilt as desired.

4. Bind the quilt with double-fold binding made with (10) 2½" × 42" binding strips.

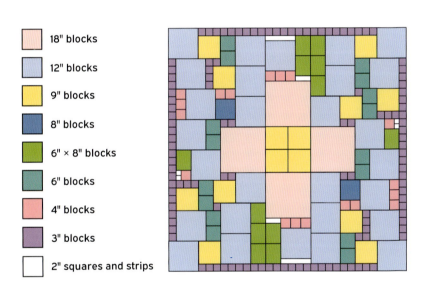

- 18" blocks
- 12" blocks
- 9" blocks
- 8" blocks
- 6" × 8" blocks
- 6" blocks
- 4" blocks
- 3" blocks
- 2" squares and strips

EXPERIENCE QUILT PLANNING OPTION

All the blocks are drafted with coordinating math, so following the same partial-seam-construction principles, many different layouts are possible. To provide a place to start varying the design, here's a diagram of this quilt showing the block placement by size. Within each block size, move blocks around, use more of your favorite blocks, **or** you can also substitute your *own blocks of the same size* into the plan!

This helpful chart gives quilt size layouts per block size. Use it as a reference to adapt many of the blocks / quilt patterns in this book for common quilt sizes.

	6" BLOCKS	9" BLOCKS	12" BLOCKS
Throw size	100 blocks, 10 × 10 60" × 60" **OR** 120 blocks, 10 × 12 60" × 72"	49 blocks, 7 × 7 63" × 63" **OR** 120 blocks, 10 × 12 60" × 72"	25 blocks, 5 × 5 60" × 60" **OR** 30 blocks, 5 × 6 60" × 72"
Twin size	192 blocks, 12 × 16 72" × 96"	88 blocks, 8 × 11 72" × 99"	48 blocks, 6 × 8 72" × 96"
Queen size	256 blocks, 16 × 16 96" × 96"	121 blocks, 11 × 11 99" × 99"	64 blocks, 8 × 8 96" × 96"
King size	288 blocks, 18 × 16 108" × 96"	132 blocks, 12 × 11 108" × 99"	72 blocks, 9 × 8 108" × 96"

The Experience Quilt Construction

Spirited Star Quilt

96" × 96"

Four Spirited Star blocks create a ring when rotated and sewn together. Nine of these four-block rings make up this quilt, with one of the pieced strips from the block repeating through the border.

Spirited Star Quilt by Victoria Findlay Wolfe, quilted by Shelly Pagliai, 2023

MATERIALS & CUTTING

Background & Borders

5½ yards *light print*
108 squares 2½" × 2½"
36 (**A**) rectangle 4½" × 6½"
36 (**B**) rectangle 3½" × 2½"
48 (**F**) rectangle 5½" × 4½"
8 strips 12½" × WOF (width of fabric) to cut border pieces:
  (2) 24½" long, (10) 20½" long, (2) 12½" long, (2) 8½" long.

Star Points

¼ yard each of *9 brown prints*
from each print, cut **16** squares 2⅞" × 2⅞", cut in half diagonally (32 triangles)

Star Centers

¼ yard (**or fat eighth**) **each of** *9 prints*
from each print, cut **4** squares 4½" × 4½"

Corner Squares

⅛ yard each of *18 light prints*
from each print, cut **2** squares 4½" × 4½" *(+ 1–2 additional squares needed for border from 8 prints)*

Star Trail

¼ yard each of *9 bright prints*
from each print, cut **4** squares 2⅞" × 2⅞", cut in half diagonally (8 triangles)
4 (**C**) rectangles 1½" × 2½"
4 (**E**) rectangles 2½" × 4½" *(+ 1–2 additional rectangles needed for border from 8 prints)*

Background Accent I

⅛ yard each of *9 prints*
from each print, cut
4 squares 2⅞" × 2⅞", cut in half diagonally (8 triangles)
4 (**D**) rectangle 1½" × 4½" *(+ 1–2 additional rectangles needed for border from 8 prints)*

Background Accent II

⅛ yard each of *9 light prints*
2 squares 2⅞" × 2⅞", cut in half diagonally (4 triangles)
4 squares 2½" × 2½"

Background Accent III

⅛ yard each of *9 prints*
6 squares 2⅞" × 2⅞", cut in half diagonally (12 triangles)

102" × 102" piece of batting
8½ yards fabric for backing
¾ yard fabric for binding

ASSEMBLY

1. Make four Spirited Star blocks from each combination of fabrics. The only difference in these four is the different corner square fabrics—make two blocks with each corner square. See Spirited Star block instructions (p. 34).

2. Rotate each set of four blocks around their corner squares, alternating the corner square fabric to form a four-patch in the middle. Sew each four-block ring section together, pinning at all intersecting seams to match points.

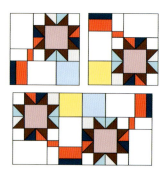

3. Arrange the ring sections, using the quilt layout diagram as a reference.

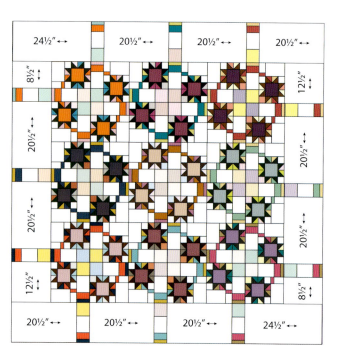

4. Sew the ring sections together in rows. Press seam allowances in one direction, alternating the direction for each row.

5. Sew the rows together. Press seam allowances to the side.

6. Determine which fabrics to cut the extra corner squares and E & D rectangles needed for the border strips by the position of the ring sections (cut one set for the ring sections on the sides of the quilt; cut two sets for the ring sections in the corners.) Sew each strip together in the same way as for the blocks.

7. Piece the 12½" wide borders together with the lengths in the order indicated on the diagram. Sew the side borders on first, then the top and bottom borders, pinning at all intersecting seams to match points.

FINISHING

1. Cut the 8½ yards of backing fabric into (3) 102" × WOF (width of fabric) panels.

   Trim the selvages from the fabric lengths. Using a ½" seam allowance, sew the panels together and trim to make a backing that measures approximately 102" × 102". Press the seams to one side.

2. Layer the quilt top, batting, and backing.

3. Quilt as desired.

4. Bind the quilt with double-fold binding made with (10) 2½" × 42" binding strips.

Loops, Lines, & Dimensions Quilt

72" × 84"

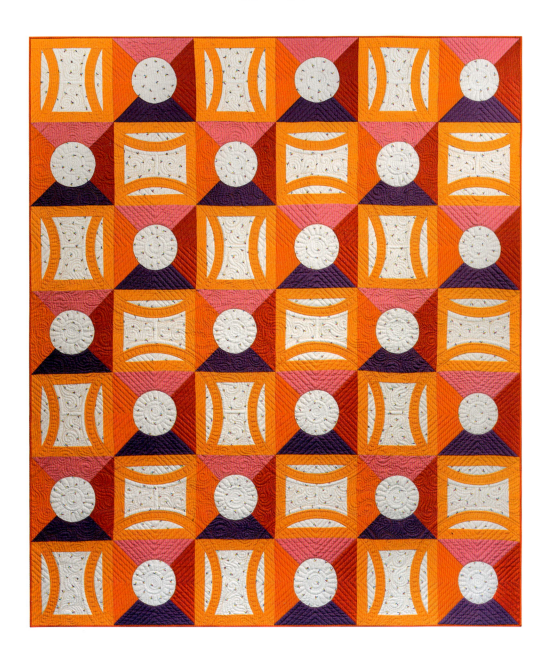

Loops, Lines, & Dimensions Quilt by Victoria Findlay Wolfe, quilted by Teresa Silva, 2023

MATERIALS

2½ yards solid light orange
2½ yards white background print
1 yard solid pink
1 yard solid medium orange
1 yard solid dark orange
1 yard solid lavender

78" × 90" piece of batting
5 yards fabric for backing
⅔ yard fabric for binding

CUTTING

From solid light orange, cut:

3 strips 9½" × WOF (width of fabric). From strips, cut **42** ring arcs.
25 strips 2" × WOF. From strips, cut **42** rectangles 2" × 12½" and **42** rectangles 2" × 9½".

From white background print, cut:

6 strips 9½" × WOF. From strips, cut **42** half melons and **21** concave centers.
21 circles, Dimensions circle template

From each of 4 solid-color fabrics, pink, medium orange, dark orange, and lavender, cut:

6 strips 4½" × WOF. From strips, cut **21** side pieces, Dimensions side template.

ASSEMBLY

1. Make (21) Loops & Lines blocks with solid light-orange and white background print pieces, following Loops & Lines block instructions (p. 100). Make (21) Dimensions blocks with the white background circles and pink, medium-orange, dark-orange, and lavender side pieces, following Dimensions block instructions (p. 158).

make 21   make 21

2. Arrange the blocks, rotating them as shown, using the quilt layout diagram as a reference—6 blocks × 7 blocks.

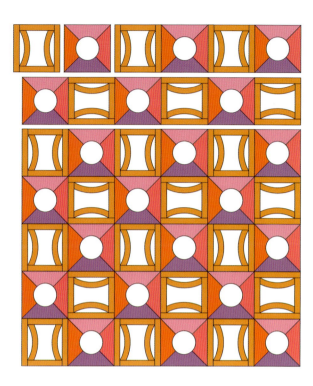

3. Sew the blocks together in rows. Press seam allowances in one direction, alternating the pressing direction for each row.

4. Sew the rows together to complete the quilt top. Press seam allowances to the side.

FINISHING

1. Cut the 5 yards of backing fabric into (2) 90" × WOF (width of fabric) panels.

   Trim the selvages from the fabric lengths. Using a ½" seam allowance, sew the panels together and trim to make a backing that measures approximately 78" × 90". Press the seams to one side.

2. Layer the quilt top, batting, and backing.

3. Quilt as desired.

4. Bind the quilt with double-fold binding made with (8) 2½" × 42" binding strips.

Loops & Lines Quilt

108" × 96"

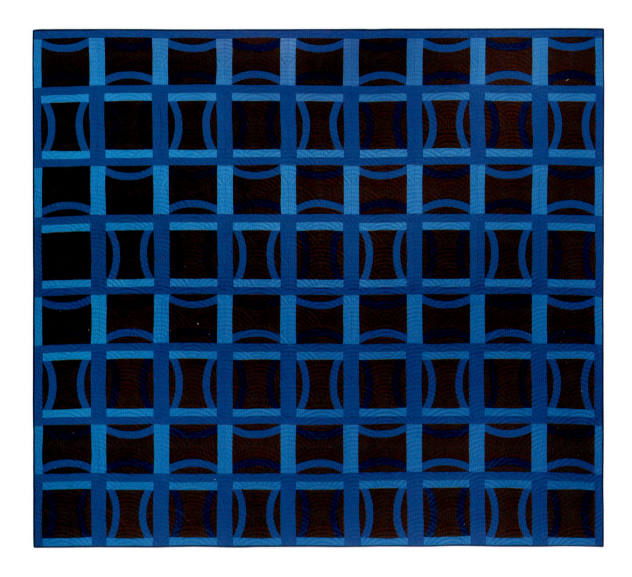

Loops & Lines Quilt by Victoria Findlay Wolfe, quilted by Julie Hirt, 2023

MATERIALS

4 yards solid medium blue
2¼ yards solid light blue
1½ yards solid dark blue
4 yards solid brown

114" × 102" piece of batting
8½ yards fabric for backing
1 yard fabric for binding

CUTTING

From solid medium blue, cut:

5 strips 9½" × WOF (width of fabric). From strips, cut **72** ring arcs.

48 strips 2" × WOF. From strips, cut **144** rectangles 2" × 12½".

From solid light blue, cut:

36 strips 2" × WOF. From strips, cut **144** rectangles 2" × 9½".

From solid dark blue, cut:

5 strips 9½" × WOF. From strips, cut **72** ring arcs.

From solid brown, cut:

15 strips 9½" × WOF. From strips, cut **144** half melons and **72** concave centers.

ASSEMBLY

1. Make (36) Loops & Lines blocks with (1) medium-blue and (1) dark-blue ring arc in each, following Loops & Lines block instructions (p. 100). Make (18) Loops & Lines blocks with (2) medium-blue ring arcs. Make (18) blocks with (2) dark-blue ring arcs.

make 36

make 18

make 18

2. Arrange the blocks, using the quilt layout diagram as a reference—9 blocks × 8 blocks. For rows with horizontal ring arcs, blocks with medium-blue/dark-blue ring arcs are rotated 180 degrees every other block. For rows with vertical ring arcs, alternate blocks with medium-blue ring arcs and blocks with dark-blue ring arcs.

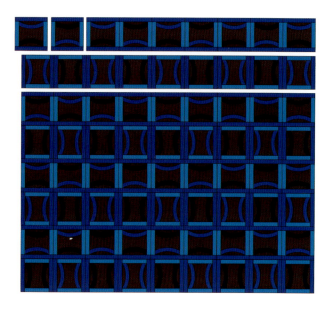

3. Sew the blocks together in rows. Press seam allowances in one direction, alternating the pressing direction for each row.

4. Sew the rows together to complete the quilt top. Press seam allowances to the side.

FINISHING

1. Cut the 8½ yards of backing fabric into (3) 102" × WOF (width of fabric) panels.

   Trim the selvages from the fabric lengths. Using a ½" seam allowance, sew the panels together and trim to make a backing that measures approximately 114" × 102". Press the seams to one side.

2. Layer the quilt top, batting, and backing.

3. Quilt as desired.

4. Bind the quilt with double-fold binding made with (11) 2½" × 42" binding strips.

Floris Ombre Quilt

96" × 96"

Five steps of color—dark (solid green 1) to light (solid green 5)—for the green leaves in these Floris blocks creates a warm ombre effect for this four-block quilt. A secondary design in the quilt emerges by rotating the blocks in each row.

Floris Ombre Quilt by Victoria Findlay Wolfe, quilted by Julie Hirt, 2023

MATERIALS & CUTTING

Flower Centers

From **1¼ yards** *pink print*, cut:
16 strips 2½" × WOF (width of fabric). From strips, cut **256** squares 2½" × 2½".

Flowers

From **3¼ yards** *yellow print*, cut:
16 strips 2½" × WOF. From strips, cut **256** squares 2½" × 2½".
16 strips 4½" × WOF. From strips, cut **256** rectangles 2½" × 4½".

Backgrounds *using Floris block templates*

From **3 yards** *solid light blue*, cut:
22 strips 4½" × WOF. From strips, cut **256** left triangles and **256** right triangles.

Leaves *using Floris block templates*

From **¾ yard** *solid green 1 (darkest)*, cut:
4 strips 4½" × WOF. From strips, cut **44** left triangles and **44** right triangles.
3 strips 2½" × WOF. From strips, cut **44** squares 2½" × 2½".

From **¾ yard** *green 2 print*, cut:
4 strips 4½" × WOF. From strips, cut **44** left triangles and **44** right triangles.
3 strips 2½" × WOF. From strips, cut **44** squares 2½" × 2½".

From **1¼ yards** *solid green 3*, cut:
6 strips 4½" × WOF. From strips, cut **68** left triangles and **68** right triangles.
5 strips 2½" × WOF. From strips, cut **68** squares 2½" × 2½".

From **1½ yards** *solid green 4*, cut:
7 strips 4½" × WOF. From strips, cut **76** left triangles and **76** right triangles.
5 strips 2½" × WOF. From strips, cut **76** squares 2½" × 2½".

From **½ yard** *solid green 5 (lightest)*, cut:
2 strips 4½" × WOF. From strips, cut **24** left triangles and **24** right triangles.
2 strips 2½" × WOF. From strips, cut **24** squares 2½" × 2½".

102" × 102" piece of batting
8½ yards fabric for backing
¾ yard fabric for binding

ASSEMBLY

1. Following the Floris block directions on p. 74, make a total of 256 Floris blocks. The number of blocks needed for each shade of green is indicated below.

green 1 blocks make 44   green 2 blocks make 44   green 3 blocks make 68   green 4 blocks make 76   green 5 blocks make 24

2. For one quadrant of the quilt top, lay out (11) green 1 blocks, (11) green 2 blocks, (17) green 3 blocks, (19) green 4 blocks, and (6) green 5 blocks as shown.

make 4

3. Sew blocks into rows, pinning at seam intersections; sew rows together to create a quadrant. Press seams open. Make four quadrants with this same arrangement.

4. Arrange the four quadrants by rotating each one clockwise as you move clockwise around the quilt top.

5. Sew top quadrants together and bottom quadrants together, pressing seams open. Sew the top and bottom together, pressing seam open, to complete the quilt top.

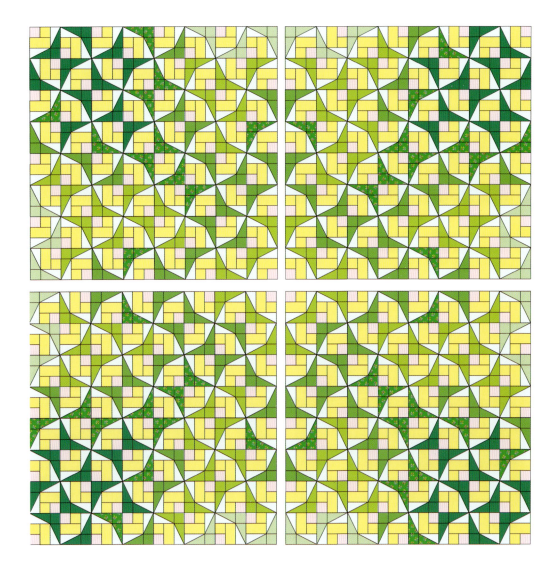

FINISHING

1. Cut the 8½ yards of backing fabric into (3) 102" × WOF (width of fabric) panels.

   Trim the selvages from the fabric lengths. Using a ½" seam allowance, sew the panels together and trim to make a backing that measures approximately 102" × 102". Press the seams to one side.

2. Layer the quilt top, batting, and backing.

3. Quilt as desired.

4. Bind the quilt with double-fold binding made with (10) 2½" × 42" binding strips.

Floris Ombre Quilt

Floris Lattice Quilt

72" × 72"

Alternating the leaf colors within each 12" Floris block works to create a striking lattice design over the quilt.

Floris Lattice Quilt by Victoria Findlay Wolfe, pieced by Jessica Scheer, quilted by Julie Hirt, 2023

MATERIALS & CUTTING

Flower Centers

¼ yard each of 7 solid-color fabrics

From 1 fabric for block A, cut:

2 strips 2½" × WOF (width of fabric). From strips, cut **24** squares 2½" × 2½".

From each of 6 fabrics for blocks B–G, cut:

2 strips 2½" × WOF. From strips, cut **20** squares 2½" × 2½".

Flowers

½ yard each of 7 red/pink/orange/yellow prints

From 1 print for block A, cut:

2 strips 2½" × WOF (width of fabric). From strips, cut **24** squares 2½" × 2½".

2 strips 4½" × WOF. From strips, cut **24** rectangles 2½" × 4½".

From each of 6 fabrics for Blocks B–G, cut:

2 strips 2½" × WOF. From strips, cut **20** squares 2½" × 2½".

2 strips 4½" × WOF. From strips, cut **20** rectangles 2½" × 4½".

Backgrounds *using Floris block templates*

1¾ yards aqua print, cut:

12 strips 4½" × WOF. From strips, cut **144** left triangles and **144** right triangles.

Leaves *using Floris block templates*

1¼ yards solid navy, cut:

6 strips 4½" × WOF. From strips, cut **72** left triangles and **72** right triangles.

5 strips 2½" × WOF. From strips, cut **72** squares 2½" × 2½".

1¼ yards navy print, cut:

6 strips 4½" × WOF. From strips, cut **72** left triangles and **72** right triangles.

5 strips 2½" × WOF. From strips, cut **72** squares 2½" × 2½".

78" × 78" piece of batting
4⅓ yards fabric for backing
⅔ yard fabric for binding

ASSEMBLY

1. Follow the Floris block directions on p. 74, arranging the blocks as for the 12" Floris block to make the needed blocks A–G shown in the diagram.

Block A make 6   Block B make 5   Block C make 5

Block D make 5   Block E make 5   Block F make 5   Block G make 5

2. Arrange the blocks, using the quilt layout diagram as a reference—6 blocks × 6 blocks. Pay attention to the direction each 12" block is rotated to form the diagonal lattice design.

3. Sew blocks into rows, pinning seam intersections; sew rows together to complete the quilt top. Press seams open.

FINISHING

1. Cut the 4⅓ yards of backing fabric into (2) 78" × WOF (width of fabric) panels.

   Trim the selvages from the fabric lengths. Using a ½" seam allowance, sew the panels together and trim to make a backing that measures approximately 78" × 78". Press the seams to one side.

2. Layer the quilt top, batting, and backing.

3. Quilt as desired.

4. Bind the quilt with double-fold binding made with (8) 2½" × 42" binding strips.

Floris Lattice Quilt

Traveling Hearts Quilt

96" × 96"

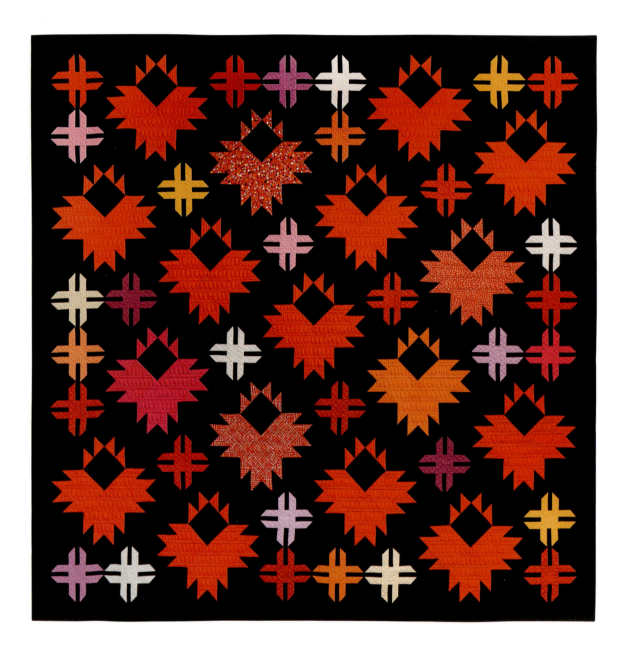

Using that partial seam knowledge, 9" and 18" blocks can float around and break free from a traditional grid layout.

Traveling Hearts Quilt by Victoria Findlay Wolfe, quilted by Teresa Silva, 2023

MATERIALS & CUTTING

Backgrounds

6½ yards of solid black fabric
for Bear Paw Heart blocks, cut:
17 squares 5½" × 5½"
85 squares 4¾" × 4¾", cut in half diagonally in both directions (340 small triangles)
34 squares 8⅛" × 8⅛", cut in half diagonally (68 setting triangles)
for 9" Transit blocks, cut:
128 squares 3½" × 3½"
128 rectangles 1¼" × 3½"
256 small squares 1⅝" × 1⅝"
for borders, cut:
10 strips 3½" × WOF (width of fabric)

Bear Paw Hearts & 9" Transit

2 yards of solid red fabric
for 12 Bear Paw Heart blocks, cut:
36 squares 5½" × 5½"
48 squares 4¾" × 4¾", cut in half diagonally in both directions (192 small triangles)

¼ yard each of 3 red prints
from each print, for 1 Bear Paw Heart block, cut:
3 squares 5½" × 5½"
4 squares 4¾" × 4¾", cut in half diagonally in both directions (16 small triangles)

⅓ yard each of solid dark-orange and solid fuchsia fabrics
from each fabric, for 1 Bear Paw Heart block, cut:
3 squares 5½" × 5½"
4 squares 4¾" × 4¾", cut in half diagonally in both directions (16 small triangles)
from each fabric, for 1 Transit block, cut:
1 square 3½" × 3½"
8 rectangles 1⅝" × 3½"

⅔ yard solid dark-red fabric
for 11 Transit blocks, cut:
11 squares 3½" × 3½"
88 rectangles 1⅝" × 3½"

¼ yard solid light-pink fabric
for 4 Transit blocks, cut:
4 squares 3½" × 3½"
32 rectangles 1⅝" × 3½"

¼ yard solid light-orange fabric
for 3 Transit blocks, cut:
3 squares 3½" × 3½"
24 rectangles 1⅝" × 3½"

⅛ yard each of 6 assorted solid pinks/oranges
from each fabric, for 2 Transit blocks, cut:
2 squares 3½" × 3½"
16 rectangles 1⅝" × 3½"

102" × 102" piece of batting
8½ yards fabric for backing
¾ yard solid black fabric for binding

ASSEMBLY

1. Make (17) Bear Paw Heart blocks, instructions on p. 60: 10 blocks with solid red and 3 blocks from red prints, 1 block solid orange, and 1 block solid fuchsia.

2. Make (32) 9" Transit blocks, instructions on p. 128: 11 blocks with solid dark red, 4 blocks with solid light pink, 3 blocks with light orange, 2 blocks each from six assorted solid pinks/oranges, and 1 block each from solid orange and solid fuchsia.

3. Arrange the blocks, using the quilt layout diagram as a reference.

4. Sew the blocks into sections indicated by the diagram. Sew a partial seam for any block ends that don't line up at the edge of the sections (stop sewing 1"–2" from the end of the shortest piece, securing with a small backstitch.) Lightly press seam allowances to one side after each seam, taking care to avoid pressing any loose parts of partial seams.

5. Starting from the bottom right corner, sew the sections together in numerical order. When adding onto a section at a partial seam, add onto the side that is a full length (both ends line up) first. Then put the other side together to close the partial seam.

6. Trim the selvages from the 3½" strips and sew the short ends together, trimming to make two borders 90½" long (sides) and two borders 96½" long (top and bottom.) Fold borders and quilt center in half to mark the centers of these long seams. Pin and sew the side borders on first, then the top and bottom borders, pressing seams toward borders.

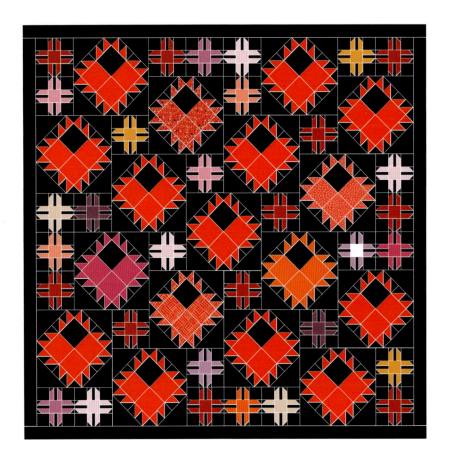

FINISHING

1. Cut the 8½ yards of backing fabric into (3) 102" × WOF (width of fabric) panels.

   Trim the selvages from the fabric lengths. Using a ½" seam allowance, sew the panels together and trim to make a backing that measures approximately 102" × 102". Press the seams to one side.

2. Layer the quilt top, batting, and backing.

3. Quilt as desired.

4. Bind the quilt with double-fold binding made with (10) 2½" × 42" binding strips.

Traveling Hearts Quilt

Facets Block Pillow
24" × 24"

MATERIALS & CUTTING
(use 6" Facets block templates)

½ yard solid aqua fabric. Cut:
- 48 rectangles
- 48 triangle A
- 96 triangle B

⅛ yard EACH of 2 light-green prints. From each print, cut:
- 2 squares
- 8 rectangles
- 8 triangle A
- 16 triangle B

⅛ yard EACH of 2 solid teal fabrics. From each fabric, cut:
- 8 rectangles
- 8 pointed rectangles

12" × 12" scrap EACH, 12 bright prints. From each fabric, cut:
- 4 rectangles
- 4 pointed rectangles

3½" × 3½" scraps, 12 bright solids. From each fabric, cut:
- 1 square

¾ yard fabric for pillow back. Cut 2 pieces 15½" × 24½".

¼ yard binding fabric. Cut 3 strips 2½" × WOF (width of fabric) (trim selvages).

26" × 26" piece of batting
26" × 26" piece of muslin (or light-color solid fabric)
Pillow form or stuffing

ASSEMBLY

1. Using the photo and diagram for color/fabric placement and following 6" Facets block instructions (p. 142), make 12 Facets blocks and 4 Facets Variation blocks.

make 4 blocks

make 12 blocks

2. Sew blocks together, 4 blocks × 4 blocks, pinning at intersections to match points.

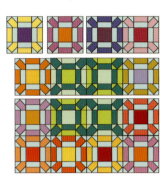

3. Layer the muslin, batting, and pillow top. Quilt by hand or machine as desired.

PILLOW FINISHING

1. On one long side of each pillow back rectangle, double-fold a small hem ⅛" – 3⁄16". Press, then topstitch in place.

2. Place pillow front and backs wrong sides together, matching outside edges and allowing the finished back hems to overlap in the middle of pillow. Sew ¼" seam around all four sides. Reinforce both sides where back pieces overlap with an extra row of stitching in the seam allowance.

3. Sew binding strips together to form one long strip. Fold wrong sides together lengthwise and press.

4. With a ¼" seam, sew the raw edges of the binding to the edges of the right side of the quilt. Turn the folded edge of the binding to the backside of the quilt and stitch in place by hand, mitering the corners.

215

Bestie Block Pillow
18" × 18"

MATERIALS & CUTTING

For 4" block pillow: use 4" Bestie block templates.

¼ yard solid aqua fabric for backgrounds. Cut **64** triangles.

6" × 6" scrap EACH of 16 bright prints for wings. From each fabric, cut **2** trapezoids.

2" × 5" scrap EACH of 16 solid fabrics for centers. From each fabric, cut **1** rectangle 1½" × 4½".

⅛ yard solid navy fabric for sashing/borders. Cut **3** strips 1¼" × WOF (width of fabric). From those strips, cut **2** lengths 8½", **3** lengths 17¼", **2** lengths 18¾".

For the 6" block pillow: use 6" Bestie block templates.

¼ yard solid aqua fabric for backgrounds. Cut **36** triangles.

8" × 8" scrap EACH, 9 bright prints for wings. From each fabric, cut **2** trapezoids.

3" × 8" scrap EACH, 9 solid fabrics for centers. From each fabric, cut **1** rectangle 2" × 6½".

For each pillow:

½ yard fabric for pillow back. Cut **2** pieces 12½" × 18¾" for 4" block pillow. Cut **2** pieces 12½" × 18½" for 6" block pillow.
¼ yard binding fabric. Cut **2** strips 2½" wide × WOF (trim selvages).
20" × 20" piece of batting
20" × 20" piece of muslin (or light-color solid fabric)
Pillow form or stuffing

ASSEMBLY

1. Using the photo and diagram for color/fabric placement and following Bestie block instructions (p. 114), make (16) 4" Bestie blocks and (9) 6" Bestie blocks.

2. For the 4" Bestie block pillow: Arrange blocks in sets of four, rotating alternating blocks as shown. Sew blocks together to make four-patch units, pinning at intersections to match points.

3. Sew an 8½" strip between the top two units and one between the bottom two units, pressing seams toward the sashing. Sew a 17¼" strip between these top and bottom sections.

Then sew the other two 17¼" strips to the top and bottom edges, pressing all seams toward the sashing. Complete the pillow top by sewing the 18¾" strips to the sides.

4. For the 6" Bestie block pillow: arrange blocks 3 × 3 as shown, rotating alternating blocks.

Sew blocks together in rows, pinning at intersections to match points. Press seam allowances to one side, alternating direction with each row. Sew rows together, again pinning to match points. Press seams to one side.

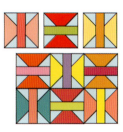

5. For both pillows: Layer the muslin, batting, and pillow top. Quilt by hand or machine as desired.

Follow pillow finishing directions for Facets Pillow, p. 215.

Jubilate Quilt

72" × 96"

Jubilate Quilt by Victoria Findlay Wolfe, quilted by Shelly Pagliai, 2023

MATERIALS & CUTTING

Background

4¼ yards solid white. Cut:
96 backgrounds
96 reverse backgrounds
96 center triangles

Swags

1¼ yards solid lavender. Cut:
96 reverse swags

Swags, Frames, Center Triangles

A-
1⅔ yards solid black. Cut:
96 swags
12 reverse frames
12 small triangles
22 center triangles

Frames, Center Triangles

B-
⅔ yard solid navy. Cut:
22 reverse frames
22 small triangles
10 center triangles

C-
⅔ yard solid dark brown. Cut:
12 frames
12 small triangles
30 center triangles

D-
½ yard solid brown. Cut:
12 frames
10 reverse frames
22 small triangles

E-
¼ yard solid dark gray. Cut:
10 reverse frames
10 small triangles

F-
⅓ yard solid gray. Cut:
10 reverse frames
10 small triangles
12 center triangles

G-
¼ yard solid pale gray. Cut:
10 frames
10 small triangles

H-
¼ yard solid green. Cut:
10 reverse frames
10 small triangles

I-
½ yard solid khaki. Cut:
10 frames
10 reverse frames
20 small triangles

J-
⅔ yard solid gray blue. Cut:
20 frames.
12 reverse frames.
32 small triangles.

K-
¼ yard solid blue. Cut:
10 frames
10 small triangles

L-
¼ yard solid pale green. Cut:
10 frames
10 small triangles

M-
¼ yard solid warm gray. Cut:
22 center triangles

N-
⅓ yard solid cream. Cut:
12 frames
12 small triangles

78" × 102" piece of batting
5¾ yards fabric for backing
¾ yard fabric for binding

Jubilate Quilt

Cutting Layouts for Jubilate Template Pieces

Note: When using fabrics with no discernable right/wrong side (such as dyed solids) one template can be used to cut each piece and its reverse.

Backgrounds and reverse backgrounds

Cut from 6½" × WOF (width of fabric) strips. Unfold each strip to yield more pieces than the folded yardage.

Swags and reverse swags

Cut from 2¾" × WOF strips.

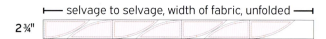

Frames and reverse frames

Cut from 4¾" × WOF strips.

Center triangles

Cut from 3½" × WOF strips.

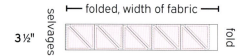

Small triangles

Cut from 2¼" × WOF strips.

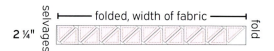

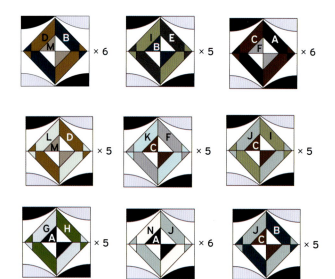

ASSEMBLY

1. Diagrams show suggested color placement and number of blocks to make from each combination. Make a total of (48) blocks following Jubilate block instructions (p. 168).

2. Arrange the blocks, using the quilt layout diagram as a reference—6 blocks × 8 blocks.

3. Sew the blocks together in rows. Press seam allowances in one direction, alternating the direction for each row.

4. Sew the rows together to complete the quilt top. Press seam allowances to the side.

Assembly, #3

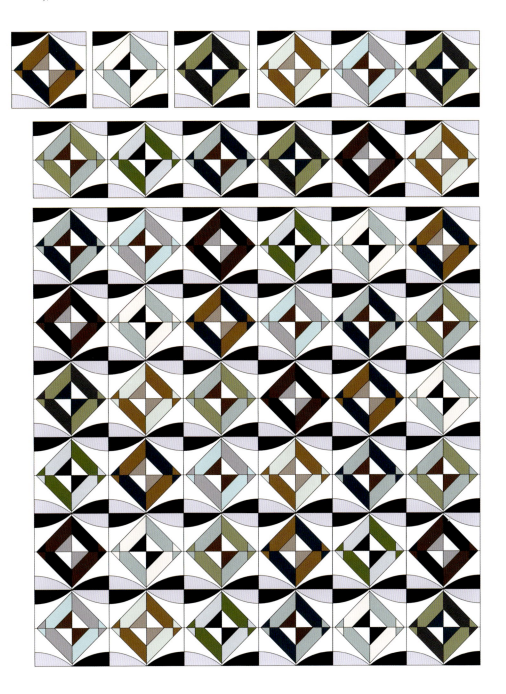

FINISHING

1. Cut the 5¾ yards of backing fabric into (2) 102" × WOF (width of fabric) panels.

   Trim the selvages from the fabric lengths. Using a ½" seam allowance, sew the panels together and trim to make a backing that measures approximately 78" × 102". Press the seam to one side.

2. Layer the quilt top, batting, and backing.

3. Quilt as desired.

4. Bind the quilt with double-fold binding made with (9) 2½" × 42" binding strips.

Jubilate Quilt

Constant Classic Quilt

60" × 72"

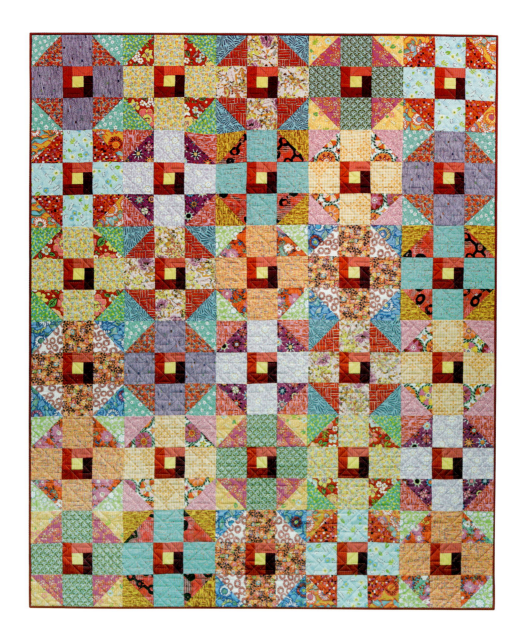

Constant Classic Quilt by Victoria Findlay Wolfe, quilted by Julie Hirt, 2023

MATERIALS

Background Half-Square Triangles ¼ yd of EACH of 10 prints

Half-Square Triangles ¼ yard of EACH of 10 prints

Squares ⅓ yard of EACH of 10 prints

Center Block Rectangles ¼ yard of EACH of four red solid-color fabrics

Center Block Squares ¼ yard yellow solid-color fabric

66" × 78" piece of batting
3⅔ yards fabric for backing
½ yard fabric for binding

CUTTING

From each of the 10 prints for background half-square triangles, cut:
1 strip 4⅞" × WOF (width of fabric). From strips, cut **6** squares 4⅞" × 4⅞".

From each of the 10 prints for half-square triangle, cut:
1 strip 4⅞" × WOF. From strips, cut **6** squares 4⅞" × 4⅞".

From each of the 10 prints for squares, cut:
2 strips 4½" × WOF. From strips, cut **12** squares 4½" × 4½".

From each of the four solids for center block rectangles, cut:
3 strips 1¾" × WOF. From strips, cut **30** rectangles 3¼" × 1¾".

From yellow solid for center block squares, cut:
2 strips 2" × WOF. From strips, cut **30** squares 2" × 2".

ASSEMBLY

1. Make (30) center units to use for all blocks. Make (3) blocks each from (10) color/fabric combinations, following Constant Classic block instructions (p. 46). Total of (30) blocks.

2. Arrange the blocks, using the quilt layout diagram as a reference—5 blocks × 6 blocks.

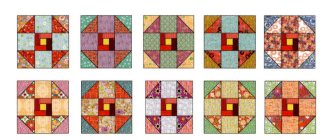

make **3** of each

3. Sew the blocks together in rows. Press seam allowances in one direction, alternating the direction for each row.

4. Sew the rows together to complete the quilt top. Press seam allowances to the side.

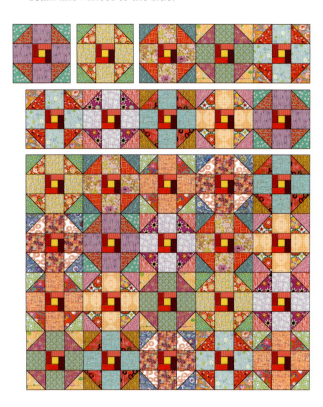

FINISHING

1. Cut the 3⅔ yards of backing fabric into (2) 66" × WOF (width of fabric) panels.

   Trim the selvages from the fabric lengths. Using a ½" seam allowance, sew the panels together and trim to make a backing that measures approximately 66" × 78". Press the seam to one side.

2. Layer the quilt top, batting, and backing.

3. Quilt as desired.

4. Bind the quilt with double-fold binding made with (7) 2½" × 42" binding strips.

Constant Classic Quilt

Facets Quilt

87 ½" × 87 ½"

These little Facets block centers are perfect for fussy cutting your favorite medallion or floral prints for a sweet tile effect. Many scrappy prints are used for this quilt, so approximate yardage amounts are given as a guide for each round of 6" Facets blocks, starting from the center of the quilt. Using one row of the block for the last round makes a beautiful scallop design in the border.

Facets Quilt by Carol Wesolik, quilted by Jane Williams, 2023

MATERIALS

Backgrounds *one white/pale print per round*

½ yard for round 2 blocks
½ yard for round 3 blocks
¾ yard for round 4 blocks
1 yard for round 5 blocks
1¼ yards for round 6 blocks
1¼ yards for round 7 blocks
½ yard for round 8 blocks

Yellow prints

½ yard for centers (rounds 1 & 7)
½ yard combined scraps of various prints for centers (round 3) and backgrounds (round 1)

Bright-pink/orange prints

¼ yard each of four prints for rectangles (round 1)

Orange prints

¾ yard of combined scraps of various prints for centers (rounds 2 & 5) and rectangles (round 2)

Blue prints

¾ yard of combined scraps of various prints for rectangles (round 3)

Red prints

1¾ yards of combined scraps of various prints for rectangles (rounds 4 & 8)

Dark-purple prints

1½ yards of combined scraps of various prints for rectangles (round 5)

Light-pink prints

1¾ yards of combined scraps of various prints for rectangles (round 6)

Aqua prints

2¼ yards of combined scraps of various prints for rectangles (round 7)

Medallion/Floral prints for fussy cutting

1 yard of combined prints for centers (rounds 4 & 6)

Solid-color triangle A for Facets Variations blocks

⅛ yard solid yellow for round 1
¼ yard solid fuchsia for round 3
¼ solid orange for round 5
⅓ yard solid magenta for round 7

94" × 94" piece of batting
8 yards fabric for backing
⅔ yard fabric for binding

CUTTING

Using 6" Facets block templates, cut for each block in rounds 1–7:

Background

4 rectangles
4 A triangles (*For Facets Variation blocks, rounds 1, 3 , 5 & 7, cut these triangles from a solid color.)
8 B triangles

Rectangles

4 rectangles
4 pointed rectangles

Center

1 square

Cut for each block in round 8:

Background

1 rectangle
4 B triangles

Rectangles (scallop edge)

1 rectangle
2 A triangles

Facets Quilt

ASSEMBLY

1. Make 6" Facets blocks and Facets Variation blocks (instructions p. 142) for each round as indicated in the diagrams.

   Round 8 blocks are the bottom row of a Facets Variation block, with the A triangles matching the rectangles / pointed rectangles.

   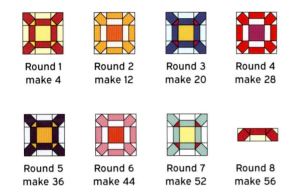

   Round 1 make 4
   Round 2 make 12
   Round 3 make 20
   Round 4 make 28
   Round 5 make 36
   Round 6 make 44
   Round 7 make 52
   Round 8 make 56

2. Arrange the blocks, using the quilt layout diagram as a reference. For the round 8 corners, cut four squares 2¼" × 2¼" from the background fabric of the round 8 blocks.

3. Sew the blocks together in horizontal rows, pinning at each seam intersection to match the points. Press seam allowances in one direction, alternating the direction for each row.

4. Pin and sew the rows together to complete the quilt top.

FINISHING

1. Cut the 8 yards of backing fabric into (3) 94" × WOF (width of fabric) panels.

   Trim the selvages from the fabric lengths. Using a ½" seam allowance, sew the panels together and trim to make a backing that measures approximately 94" × 94". Press the seams to one side.

2. Layer the quilt top, batting, and backing.

3. Quilt as desired.

4. Bind the quilt with double-fold binding made with (9) 2½" × 42" binding strips.

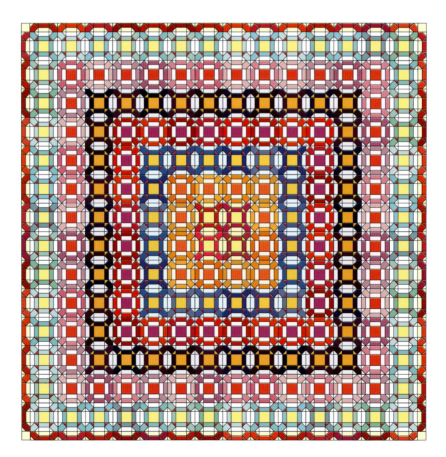

Saving Our Stories
The Work of the Quilt Alliance

Why document quilt stories? Most quilters aren't public figures or celebrities. Their quilts don't hang in museums. Quilts and their makers might have a moment of glory during show-and-tell, but otherwise they don't get paid much attention. So what's so important about these quilt stories that the Quilt Alliance has spent 30 years recording them? What's so important about the Quilters' Save Our Stories (QSOS) collection that it's housed in the Library of Congress?

Here's how we see it at the Quilt Alliance: When a quilt maker makes a quilt, they're also making quilt history, and quilt history is art history. It's women's history; it's the people's history. The QSOS collection preserves histories that would otherwise be lost, and documents artists who might otherwise never get their due.

Documenting these stories has always been at the heart of the Quilt Alliance's mission. Our organization is made up of quilters, quilt lovers, educators, small-business owners, and foundations and corporations within the quilt industry, all of whom have a vested interest in preserving quilt history and documenting quilt makers' stories. The QSOS collection serves to remind all of us that quilt making is very much alive in America—in fact, it's one of the few traditional crafts still widely practiced in this country.

Still, people are often surprised when someone mentions they make quilts. There's still an "under-the-radar" aspect to this popular craft, in spite of the fact that almost everyone has a quilt story, whether it's about a favorite childhood quilt gifted by a beloved aunt or a nine-patch that was picked up for a few dollars at Goodwill. These stories are part of our lives.

Sadly, the stories of the quilt makers often aren't. The makers of vintage and antique quilts are too often anonymous (or, as we like to say at the Quilt Alliance, currently unknown). Quilts often outlive their makers, and if the quilt doesn't have a label or a marking of some sort (a signature, for example, or initials) or some sort of documentation, the identity of a quilt's maker will too often fade away, and with it, the quilt's story.

The Quilt Alliance's oral history projects, QSOS and the Go-Tell-It! video documentary program, are grassroots efforts to document and preserve quilt makers' stories so that they'll never be forgotten. Anyone with a smartphone can interview anyone who has a quilt and a story to share. You'll find everything you need to conduct these interviews at our website, QuiltAlliance.org. We hope you'll join us in this important work.

Frances O'Roark Dowell, board member and longtime volunteer, Quilt Alliance

CLOTH CONNECTIONS

Textiles often outlive the people who make them, and more often than not, the story fades with the life of the maker. I learned this the first time when I purchased a lovely brown linen hankie marked in beautiful stitching: "Edith" on eBay. Since I don't know any Ediths personally, I enlisted my 10-year-old daughter Lilian's help to rehome the Edith hankie. We opened the city phone book and found the first Edith and mailed her the hankie with a note. I guess the subtext motivating me in suggesting this gesture was that Edith is an old-timey name, and I had a hunch that any Edith we found might be an elder who had hankie experience.

Guess what? Edith (Edie) wrote back! And along with a beautiful handwritten note, she sent us a few of her childhood hankies that were spectacular. It turned out that she was in our quilt guild (although we didn't know her), and she thought we found her in the guild directory. She told us in the note about how her mother had sent her to school each day with a hankie marked with her name, and how our hankie brought back some really nice memories.

This story speaks to the magical properties of textiles, especially the ones that include names or dates, traces of the people who once stitched it, received it, or held it tight. Edie assumed someone from our guild had sent her the package, because we often find connections within our quilting guilds and groups—a shared love of cloth, and sewing, and nostalgia.

The way I felt about owning the Edith hankie then is akin to my reaction to anonymous quilts now. I have a strong curiosity about their story and an urge to reconnect them to their maker or owner. In my case, rehoming the lost hankie led us to Edie, who provided another story—about her childhood memories, which Lil and I now preserve and share. Quilt Alliance projects have the capacity to reduce anonymity in the quilt community before that separation happens between maker and quilt. Labeling, documenting, and recording oral histories all are steps in this intervention. Saving stories starts with connections. Are you finding ways to save and share your story?

Amy Milne, executive director, Quilt Alliance

Resources

Mentioned in the Text

EVENTS, EXPERTS, AND INFO

Barn Quilt Trails
www.barnquiltinfo.com

Meg Cox
www.megcox.com

Empty Spools seminars
www.emptyspoolsseminars.com

Victoria Findlay Wolfe Quilts
www,vfwquilts.com

Gee's Bend quilters
www.geesbendquiltingretreats.com

International Quilt Market and Festival
www.quilts.com

Roderick Kiracofe
www.theamericanquilt.com

The Legacy Quilt
www.mofad.org/the-legacy-quilt

Shelly Pagliai, Prairie Moon Quilts
www.prairiemoonquilts.com

QuiltCon
www.quiltcon.com

Rebel Quilters
www.quiltshare2oblogspot.com

Rosie Lee Tompkins
www.bampfa.org/program/
virtualrosie-lee-tompkins-retrospective

Woodland Ridge Retreat
www.woodlandridgeretreat.com

ORGANIZATIONS & MUSEUMS

Acacia Network
www.acacianetwork.org

Berkeley Art Museum
www.bampfa.org

The Harlem Needle Arts (HNA)
www.harlemneedlearts.org

International Quilt Museum
www.internationalquiltmuseum.org

NYC Metro Mod Quilters
www.nycmetromodquilters.com

Project Linus
www.projectlinus.org

Quilt Alliance
www.quiltalliance.net

Quilts of Valor
www.qovf.org

BOOKS

Findlay Wolfe, Victoria. *15 Minutes of Play: Improvisational Quilts.* Concord, CA: C&T Publishing, 2012.

———. *Double Wedding Rings: Traditions Made Modern.* Concord, CA: C&T Publishing, 2015.

———. *Modern Quilt Magic: 5 Parlor Tricks to Expand Your Piecing Skills.* Concord, CA: C&T Publishing, 2017.

———. *Victoria Findlay Wolfe's Playing with Purpose: A Quilt Retrospective.* Concord, CA: C&T Publishing, 2019.

Fry, Gladys-Marie. *Stitched from the Soul: Slave Quilts from the Antebellum South.* Chapel Hill: University of North Carolina Press, 2002.

Heffley, Scott. *Bold Improvisation: Searching for African American Quilts; The Heffley Collection.* Concord, CA: C&T Publishing, 2007.

Leon, Eli. *Accidentally on Purpose: The Aesthetic Management of Irregularities in African Textiles and African-American Quilts.* Davenport, IA: Figge Art Museum, 2006.

Waldvogel, Merikay. *Soft Covers for Hard Times: Quiltmaking and the Great Depression.* Nashville: Rutledge Hill, 1990.

Templates

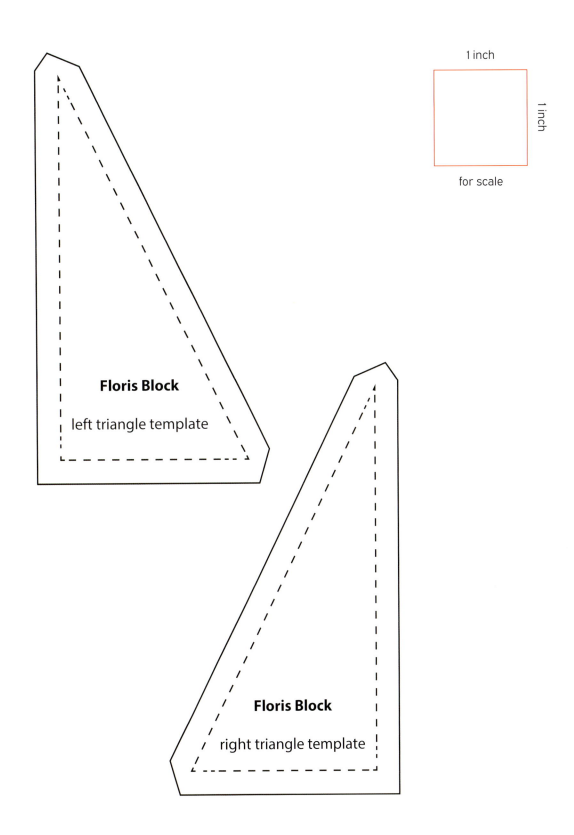

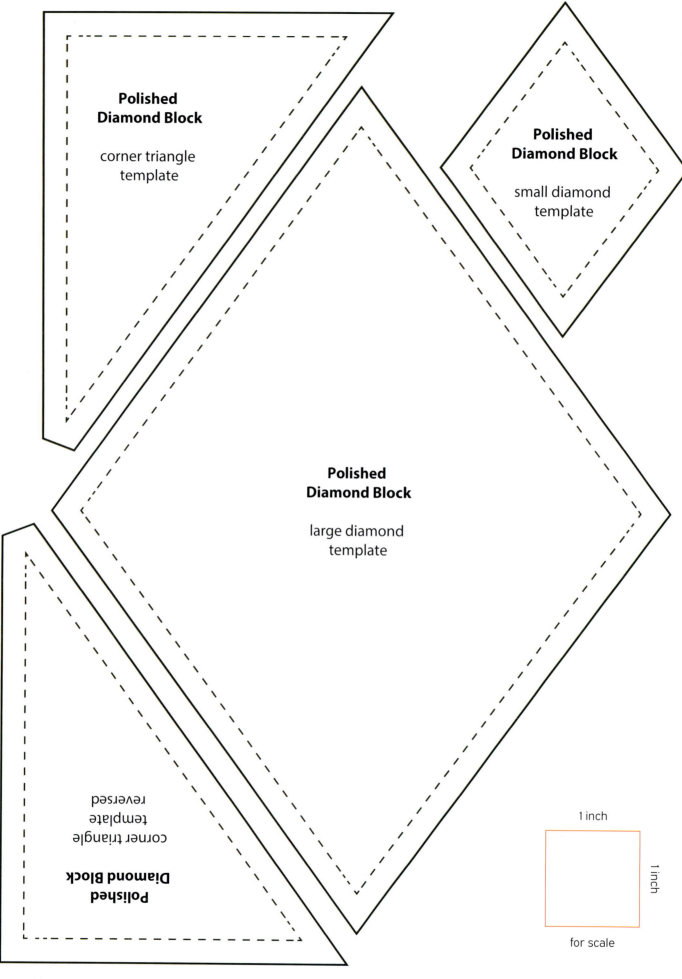

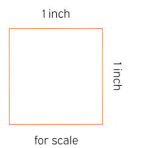
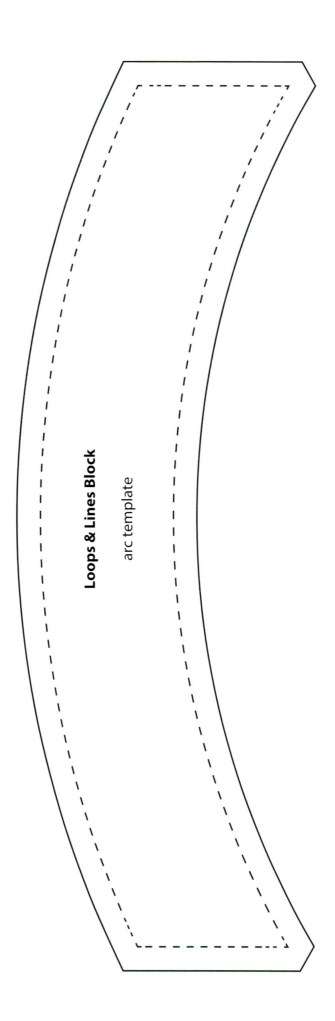

Loops & Lines Block

arc template

Templates 233

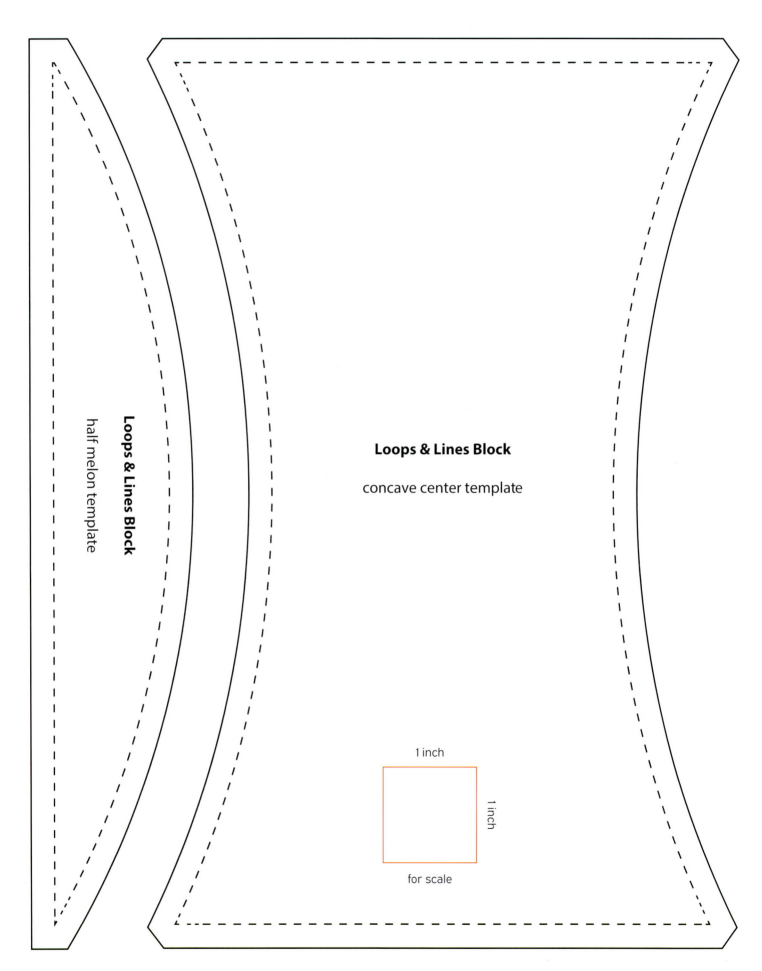

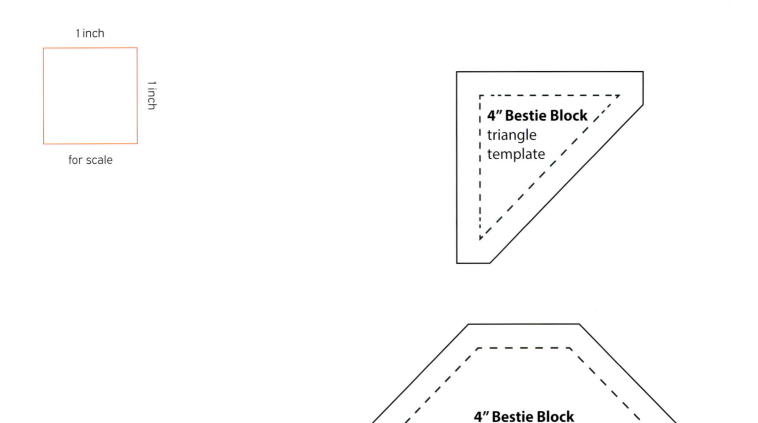
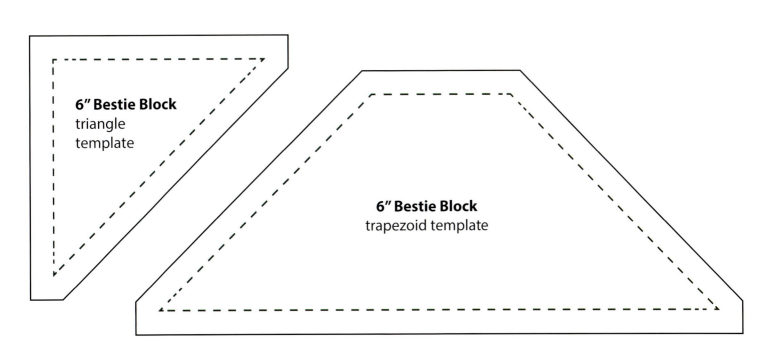

Templates 235

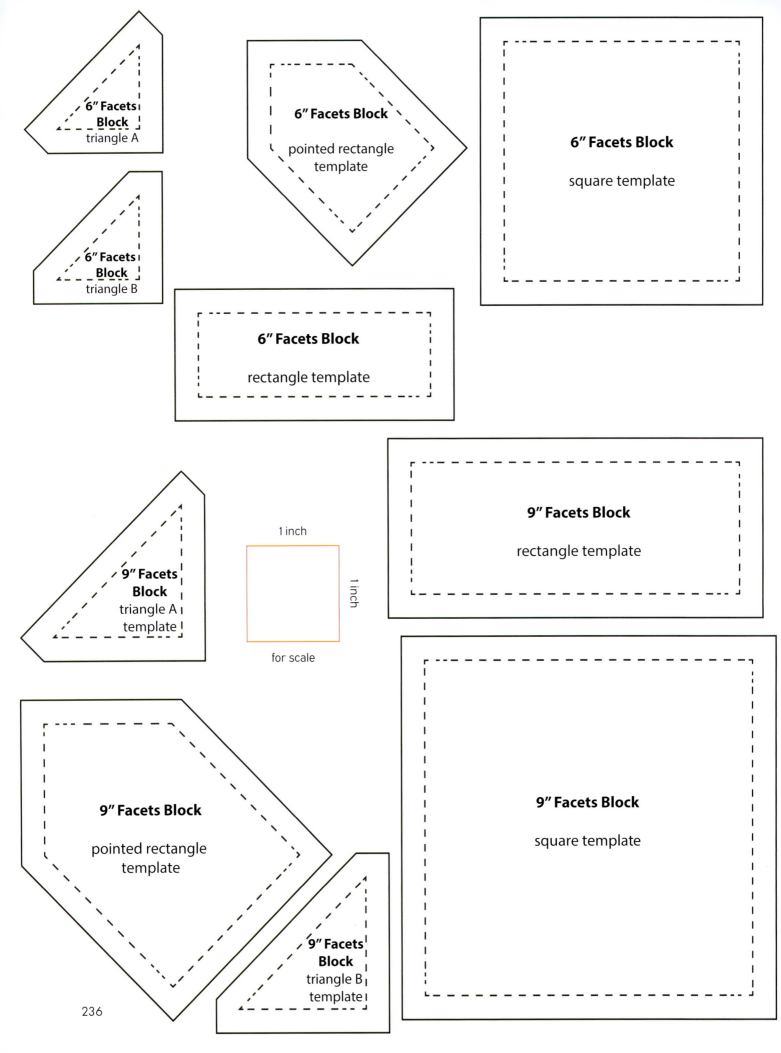

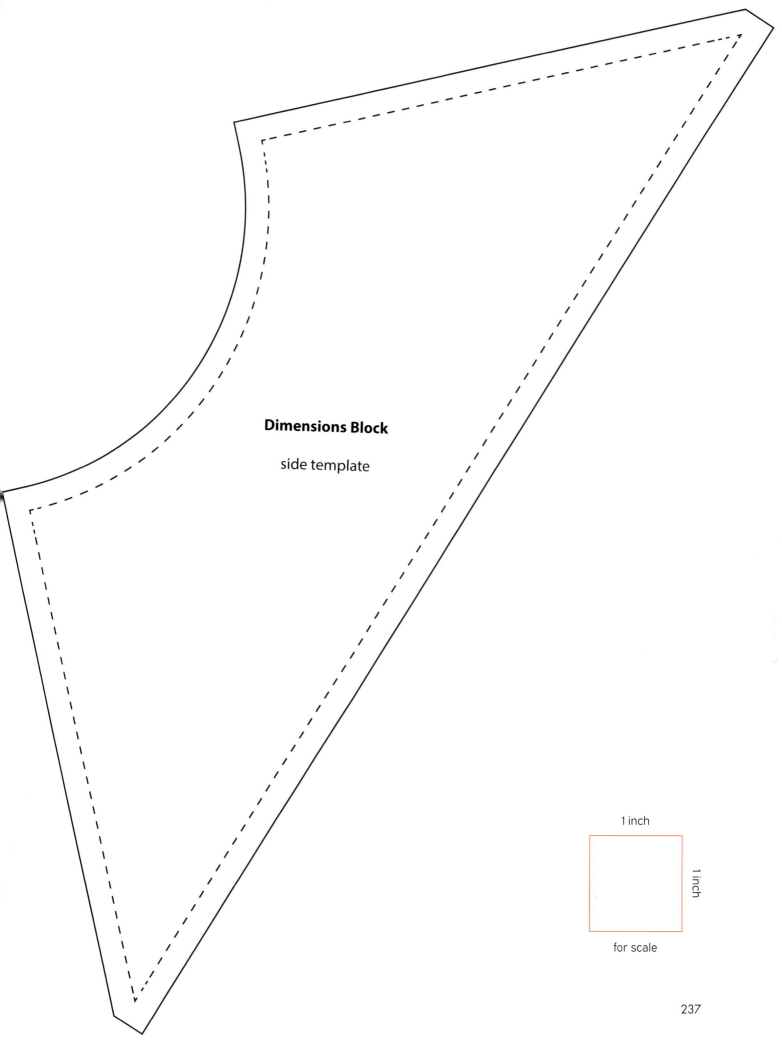

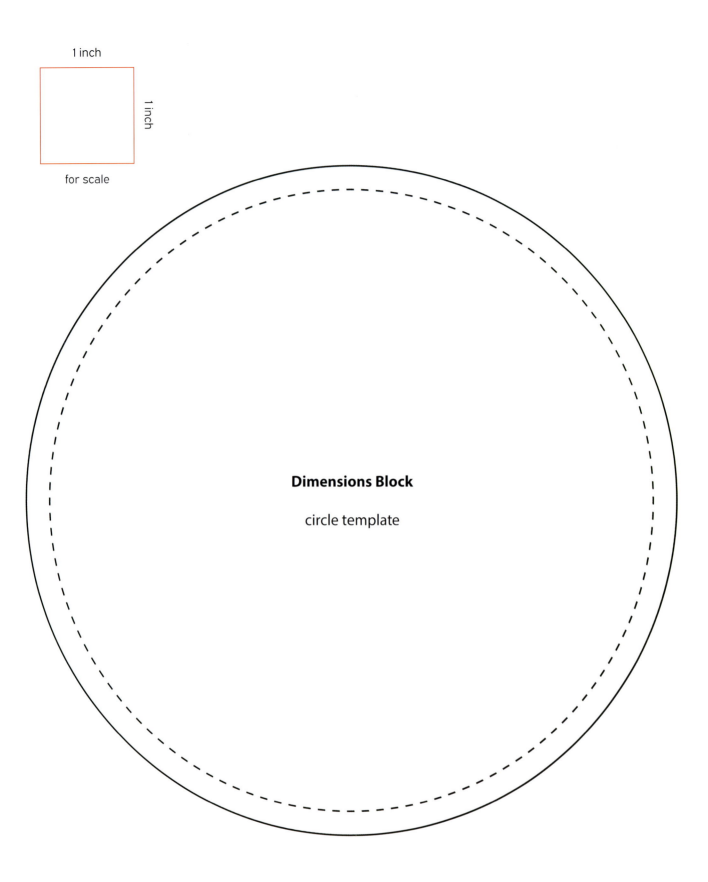

Dimensions Block

circle template

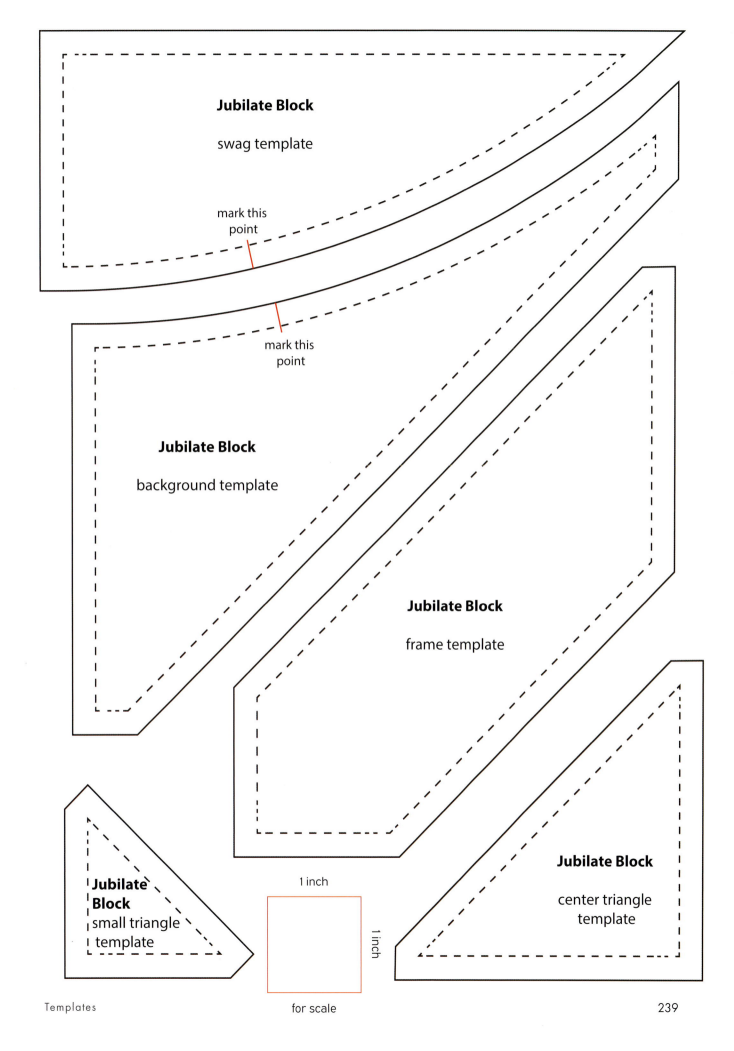

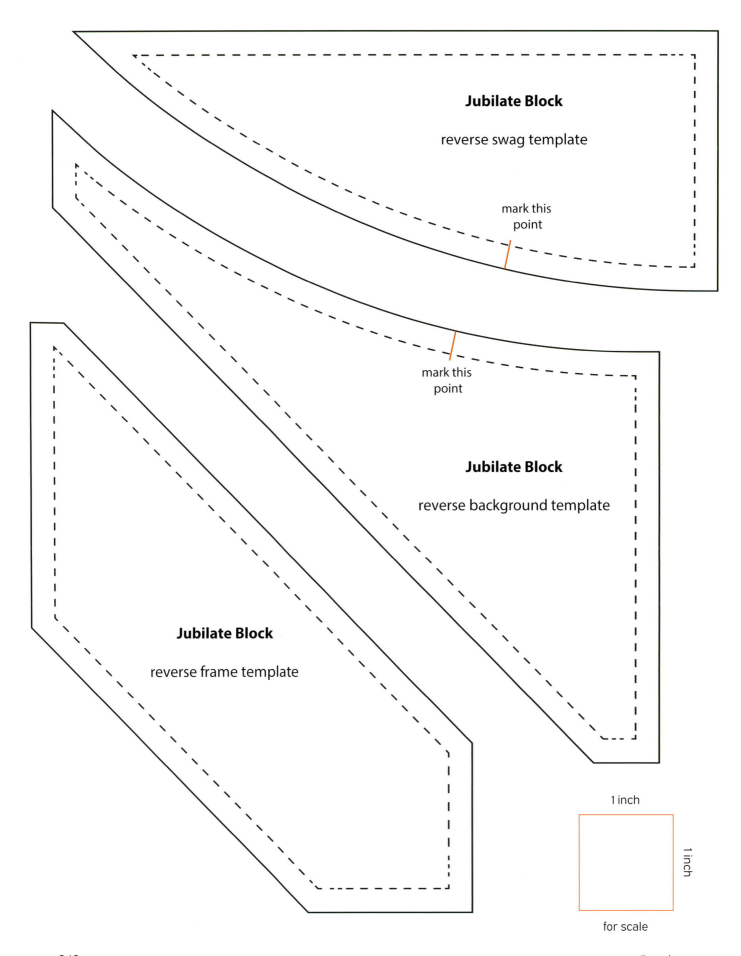